eat

NIGEL SLATER is the author of numerous best-selling books, including *Notes from the Larder, Tender,* and the James Beard Award–winning *Ripe.* He has written a column for the *Observer* for twenty years and is the host of the BBC series *Simple Suppers.* His memoir, *Toast,* won British Biography of the Year and has been adapted into a feature film. He lives in London.

Also by Nigel Slater
Notes from the Larder
Ripe
Tender
Eating for England
Toast
Appetite
Nigel Slater's Real Food
Real Cooking
The 30-Minute Cook
Real Fast Food

Photographs by Jonathan Lovekin

eat

The little book of fast food

Nigel
Slater

TEN SPEED PRESS
Berkeley

Copyright © 2013 by Nigel Slater
Photographs copyright © 2013 by Jonathan Lovekin

Published in the United States by Ten Speed Press, an imprint of
the Crown Publishing Group, a division of Random House LLC,
a Penguin Random House Company, New York.
www.crownpublishing.com
www.tenspeed.com

Ten Speed Press and the Ten Speed Press colophon are
registered trademarks of Random House LLC.

Originally published in hardcover in Great Britain by Fourth
Estate, a division of HarperCollins Publishers, London, in 2013.

Library of Congress Cataloging-in-Publication Data
Slater, Nigel.
  Eat : the little book of fast food / Nigel Slater ; photographs by
Jonathan Lovekin.
     pages cm
1. Quick and easy cooking. I. Title.
  TX833.5.S5896 2014
  641.5'12—dc23

                    2014017001

Hardcover ISBN: 978-1-60774-726-0
eBook ISBN: 978-1-60774-727-7

Printed in China

Cover design by David Pearson and Toni Tajima
Interior Design by David Pearson and Chloe Rawlins
Production by Anitra Alcantara

10 9 8 7 6 5 4 3 2 1

First U.S. Edition

For James Thompson

Contents

A quick guide by main ingredient

Meat and Poultry

bacon and pancetta

beef

chicken

duck

lamb

Vegetables

Beans

fava beans

peas

Greens

asparagus

broccoli

cabbage

kale

leeks

Roots

And all the rest

Fruit

Eggs and cheese

Leftovers

Acknowledgments

Early in 1991, I received a letter from Louise Haines, from the publisher Michael Joseph, inquiring whether I had ever considered writing a book. She had read a piece I had written in a magazine and wondered whether we could meet up. I replied that I was flattered and grateful but felt that writing a book was beyond me. Two days later she had talked me into lunch. A meal at which we hatched the idea for my first book, *Real Fast Food*, which was published in autumn 1992. Twenty-one years, ten cookbooks, a memoir, a collection of essays, and a change of publisher behind us, she remains my editor. I can never thank her enough.

Louise, this book is for you.

To: James Thompson, for his endless inspiration, wisdom, support, and friendship. Without you there would be no books, no television series, and my life wouldn't be half as much fun. Thank you, sir, for everything.

My gratitude and love also goes to Victoria Barnsley, Jonathan Lovekin, Allan Jenkins, Ruaridh Nicoll, Gareth Grundy, Michelle Kane, Georgia Mason, Olly Rowse, Jane Middleton, Annie Lee, David Pearson, Gary Simpson, Araminta Whitley, Rosemary Scoular, Sophie Hughes, Richard Stepney at Fourth Floor, Rob Watson, and everyone at ph9, and Dalton Wong and George Ashwell at Twenty Two Training. Thank you too to Jenny Zarins for allowing us to use her thoughtful portrait of me. And a big shout-out to everyone at the *Observer* and all my followers on Twitter @nigelslater. Thank you one and all.

Introduction

Sometimes we cook purely for the pleasure of it, understanding the provenance of our ingredients, choosing them with great care, thoughtfully taking them on the journey from shop to plate. We seek out the perfect recipe and take our time, lovingly preparing our dinner from scratch. There are times when we might want to take the whole business even more seriously, meeting those who produced it or, if we have the space, growing some of it for ourselves. We want to consider it, discuss it, perhaps even write about it and photograph it.

But sometimes, we just want to eat.

This little book is for those times. The days when we have barely an hour to cook. The times we just want something delicious on a plate at the end of our working day. Yes, we can phone for a pizza or for Chinese or Indian takeout. We can drop by that Vietnamese place on the way home or pick up a ready-made microwavable delight from the supermarket. But as much as I enjoy the odd take-out meal, I have always found dinner is more life-enhancing when

I have done more than open a box or pick up the phone. There is much pleasure in making dinner at home when we have cooked something, however quickly, for ourselves or for someone else. That is why I have written this book and why its subtitle is *The Little Book of Fast Food*. A collection of recipes, most of which you can have on the table in less than an hour.

By "fast" I do not mean thoughtless or careless. There is great joy to be had in a perfectly cooked steak, its fat crisping lightly on the grill; a single fillet of spanking-fresh fish singing to itself, quietly, in butter; a baked potato whose flesh has been mashed and freckled with rust-red, fat-peppered chorizo. Simple things, done well. Go up a notch and there is a thin, gold-and-white frittata of goat cheese; a light chicken ragù with thyme and green onion; or a broth made with pork ribs and dark stars of anise. Even at its most complex, a Thai vegetable curry is made in minutes once you have pureed the lemongrass, ginger, chiles, garlic, and cilantro to a yellow-green paste in the food processor. Making yourself and others something good to eat can be so little trouble and so much pleasure. And much more satisfying than coming home to a meal in a box.

This book

Twenty-one years ago, I wrote my first book, *Real Fast Food*, a collection of ideas and recipes for something to eat that you could get on the table within half an hour or so. Still in print, it is a book of which I am very fond and I wish it well, but looking at those 350 or so recipes twenty years on, I realize how much our everyday eating has changed. How once unusual ingredients are now accessible in every supermarket; how our recipes are more adventurous; the way fresh ingredients are now essential and once frowned-upon shortcuts are now used without apology. *Real Fast Food* is still relevant, but our eating has moved on. What seemed new and interesting two decades ago is now everyday. The speeded-up variations of well-known classics still stand, but there are several recipes that now seem somewhat naive, others that are no longer to my taste (we move on), and, if truth be told, there are one or two that should probably never have been there in the first place.

Although I am far from the most prolific of writers, I have written ten or so books since then, including one or two hefty tomes. For some time now I have wanted to return to the subject of fast food, to update that dear little book and bring it in line with modern eating. That is what you have in your hands. A little book of straightforward, contemporary recipes, quick or particularly easy to get to the table. A collection of recipes that are fast, simple, and, I hope, fun.

The recipes

I have every respect for the time-honored recipe. Those faultless blueprints whose every detail must be adhered to. I appreciate the classic dishes and prefer them to be carried out in their original style rather than tweaked and reinvented. That said, I have no wish to eat as if the clocks have stopped; life is too short to attempt perfection every day and to be inhibited by someone else's set of rules. Cooking should, surely, be a lighthearted, spirited affair, alive with invention, experimentation, appetite, and a sense of adventure.

The recipes here are straightforward and within the grasp of most of us. I would like to think that many of them will work for those who have never cooked anything in their lives. It is not a book of detailed, pedantic, obsessively honed directions. Written in a short style, they are, I hope, both practical and inspirational. Opposite many of the recipes are ideas that have bounced off them, a scattering of notes, suggestions, and narrative recipes that might also interest you. Think of them as little extras.

The recipes are generally for two, but they are easy enough to double up. The stumbling blocks of increasing the quantities of ingredients such as gelatin and yeast have no place in this book. Most of the ingredients are fresh, but I have taken a few shortcuts, such as using canned beans rather than the dried sort that need soaking and long cooking; the occasional sheet of frozen puff pastry; a tub of decent mayonnaise, and even, on a couple of occasions, the ready-made béchamel sauce that you can get in aseptic package from some groceries and delis. These are shortcuts I find useful for everyday cooking.

The form of the recipes is new. Written in the style of an extended tweet, they are no dogged "1-2-3" sets of instructions. The ingredients lists are next to a picture of the finished dish, both at the top of the method so you can see, at a glance, what you will need and then, in more detail, within the method. It is simple enough to get used to.

Some of the ideas in this book are updated recipes from *Real Fast Food*, others are from my "Midweek Dinners" column in the Sunday *Observer* magazine, and others still started life as tweets to my Twitter followers. Others still have been developed especially for the book by me and James Thompson over the last couple of years. Working in my kitchen at home, we have tested every recipe at least twice and cooked them for photography. They are not all thirty-minute wonders. A few are special-occasion dinners for when you have friends over, and some require minimal preparation but take a full hour or more of unattended cooking in the oven, but the bulk are neat little dinners you can have on the table in half an hour or so and probably even quicker when you have made them once or twice.

We are not chasing perfection here. This is simply a collection of suggestions for something you might like to make for dinner. Just straightforward, delicious cooking. For the times we just want to eat.

Nigel Slater
London, September 2013

www.nigelslater.com
@nigelslater

A note on the US edition

In editing this book for an American audience, we sought to do two things: one, to make it as much a treasure trove of information, inspiration, and solid cooking advice for Americans as it is for its original British audience; and two, to retain the book's engaging style and tone. To that end, the recipes and cooking instructions have been Americanized, so that ingredients, terminology, and measurements are familiar to US readers. We have retained the metric measures from the original edition. Any errors or omissions belong to the American publisher, Ten Speed Press.

A small number of ingredients used in these recipes are unfamiliar or hard to find in the States. **Black garlic** is a fermented garlic that can be found at most specialty grocery stores. In recipes that call for **ready-made béchamel** sauce, Aunt Penny's white sauce could be used; it is also quite simple to make your own béchamel sauce. **Potted shrimp** packs small cooked shrimp in a spiced butter, similar to potted meat. If you can't find it at your specialty grocery store, you could make your own using raw shrimp, butter, and herbs. Red snapper is an acceptable alternative to **red mullet**, a light-pink fish with a delicate, white flesh.

In the hand

There is an intimacy involved in eating food while holding it in your hands. An intimacy you cannot get from the cold steel of a knife and fork or even a pair of wooden chopsticks. The tactile quality of food in the hands is something we get from a sandwich or a wrap (a floury roll; the charcoal dust left on our fingers from a torn piece of warm roti; the cool moistness of a rice wrapper), yet it is a way of life for some cultures, which long ago embraced the art of hand-to-mouth eating.

It is convenient to contain most handheld food in an edible wrapper—a dough of some sort. It protects our hands from the hot, messy food. A slice cut from a sourdough loaf, a baguette with a shattered crust, a flour-dusted bun, a puckered wrap, an ice cream cone, a doughy roti, rye crispbread, or thin, skin-like rice wrapper all serve the same purpose. We get to enjoy not only the filling but its wrapper as well. A wrapper that in some cases is warm to the touch and has partially soaked up the moisture from the filling.

The sandwich can be anything from a diminutive, accurately cut cucumber triangle to a doorstop bacon sandwich the size of an outstretched palm. Matching the bread to the filling can be state of the art or potluck, depending on the day. Carefully considered or thrown together, a homemade sandwich rarely fails to hit the spot. Rough pork rillettes on sourdough, goat cheese on walnut bread, and bacon on white sliced bread are among my desert-island sandwiches, and yes, I do plan for them when I'm shopping. But most are constructed in a somewhat more laissez-faire manner, which is why I have eaten salt beef on sourdough and Caerphilly cheese on a flat English muffin. (Both good, by the way.)

My rule of thumb is the softer the filling, the more suited it is to a crisp wrapping and vice versa. Which is why silkily wrapped rice paper rolls work so well with their crunchy cucumber and carrot filling and why smoked salmon and soft cream cheese are ideal for chewy bagels. It may also explain the heaven that is ripe Brie with a crackling baguette.

A sandwich needs some form of lubricant. This can be as off the cuff as a trickle of olive oil or as lavish as herb-flecked mayonnaise. It can bring heat (mustard, horseradish, or wasabi) or be something more bland altogether, such as *fromage frais*. Yes, the lubricant—butter, hummus, creamed avocado, goat cheese, mayonnaise, jam, honey, peanut butter—needs to work with the filling, but there is plenty of room to experiment. Wasabi and smoked salmon works for me, as does mayonnaise with crisp smoked bacon. Whatever works. We probably shouldn't get too precious about a sandwich, but that needn't mean we can be flippant about it either.

I must mention the burger. From the Big Mac to the now-ubiquitous gourmet burger, the idea of a meat patty held in some sort of bun has long had our attention. The patty is usually pork or beef, but I make them from lamb too, often with cumin and mint, and from sausage meat, mashed beans, and shredded vegetables flavored with mustard seed. The meat can be pure and lightly seasoned or tarted up with an entire spice rack. Both have their moments.

In its purest form, a sandwich is something you often make for yourself rather than for someone else. The bread and its filling are ours and ours alone, and we can do as we please. There are no rules. Bread that is less than perfectly fresh can be toasted; fillings can be classic (Cheddar and coarse chutney; roast beef and horseradish) to adventurous (salmon, wasabi, and grilled bacon; goat cheese, peach, and black pepper) to downright bizarre. It can be browned in a panini press or in a film of butter in a shallow pan. Eaten hot, when the melted cheese forms burning strings, or chilled, with ice-cold radishes, cucumber, and iceberg lettuce as crisp as broken glass.

The open sandwich has much to commend it. The filling is allowed to tempt the eye more than when it is held captive between two pieces of bread, and it can be more generous too. But a knife and fork are generally involved, taking away that all-important, though far from essential, tactility. An open sandwich—buttery yellow lettuce, smoked trout, dill mayonnaise, and cucumber on rye—was one of the first recipes I tweeted. It remains a favorite summer lunch.

I still stand by many of the sandwiches in my first book, *Real Fast Food* (Michael Joseph, 1992): thinly sliced cold roast pork with sea salt, smashed crackling, and mayonnaise; bread spread with anchovy paste and Camembert, toasted till the cheese runs; the bacon sandwich made with white sliced bread; even the pita bread stuffed with fried leftover potatoes, garam masala, and basil vinaigrette, despite the leap of faith you need to take to make it.

We all have our favorites. The homemade sandwich is a friend who rarely lets us down. Here are a few of my favorites, from the simplest to the most extravagant, that continue, year in, year out, to save my soul.

Roasted zucchini and feta

Slice small zucchini lengthwise—longer ones may be better cut into rounds—then put them in a small roasting pan. Toss with olive oil, salt, pepper, and a little crushed garlic. Roast till soft and sweet. Crumble over a little feta, then pile onto a crisp roll or serve as a warm open sandwich.

Roasted vegetables, garlic mayo. The warm, sweet breeze of basil

Slice eggplant, tomatoes, and zucchini, toss them in plenty of olive oil, then season with lots of garlic, black pepper, salt, and finely chopped rosemary. Roast till everything is very soft. Chop a handful of basil leaves, stir them into mayonnaise, and beat in some of the garlicky juices from the roasting pan. Stop before it curdles. Slather the basil mayo over crusty bread, then pile on the vegetables.

The comfort of carbs
Slice leftover new potatoes into thick coins. Fry them in butter and a little oil till they are lightly crisp and golden. Spread mayonnaise thickly onto your bread and pile the hot potatoes onto it. (I like to add chopped dill to this one.)

The Italian
Paper-thin air-dried ham and soft, flour-dusted, airy bread such as ciabatta. I have been known to tuck in a basil leaf or two. You can brush the cut bread with olive oil, but the holes prevent the inclusion of any sort of spread.

A few ideas inspired by the burger

Steak sandwich

A flash-fried thin steak. Crisp baguette. Mustard. Mayonnaise. The trick is to slice the bread and press the cut side down into the steak pan, wiping up all the juices with the bread, before adding the mustard, slathering with mayonnaise, and tucking the steak in. It's the pan juices that make it.

Buttery leeks and chicken burger

Buy ground chicken, or better still grind your own, so you can include the skin. Slice a green onion and fry in oil and butter, then add chopped sage, a little garlic, and leeks, finely shredded. Let them soften, slowly, under a lid, till they are bright green, satin soft, and buttery. Add the ground chicken and cook briefly before making into patties and frying in a nonstick pan until golden and sticky. Slather short lengths of crisp baguette with mayonnaise, then use to sandwich the burgers.

Breakfast Burger

sausages, bacon, bagels, tomatoes, cheese

Slit the skin of **3 herby fresh sausages**, remove the meat, and put it into a mixing bowl. Chop **2½ ounces (75g) bacon**, mix it with the sausage, then roll into two plump patties.

Using a nonstick pan covered with a lid, cook the burgers in **a little oil** over low to moderate heat. Turn each burger several times during cooking, until they have developed a sticky exterior.

Split and toast **a couple of bagels**, place **a couple of slices of large, ripe tomato** and the burgers on the bottom halves, add **a few slices of interesting cheese**, and briefly place under a hot broiler till the cheese has melted. Top with the other halves of the bagels.

For 2. Soft bun. Herby sausage. Smoked bacon. Melting cheese. Happy weekend.

A couple of ideas for poultry burgers

Chicken burger with lemon and tarragon

I can't get enough of these; they're one of my favorite recipes in the book.

Put 14 ounces (400g) chicken breasts, with their skin, in a food processor. Add a good handful of tarragon leaves, the zest and juice of a small to medium lemon, a clove of garlic, salt, pepper, and 4 heaping tablespoons of dried bread crumbs (I use panko). Process to a coarse paste but stop before the mixture becomes gluey. Heat a fine layer of olive oil in a shallow nonstick pan, then shape the mixture into about 6 patties and fry for 10 minutes, turning gently, till golden.

The Christmas burger

Fresh white and dark turkey meat, including the skin for succulence, sausage meat (I generally work with a balance of half turkey to half sausage meat), a few chopped fresh or frozen cranberries, fresh thyme, salt, and black pepper. Puree, then flatten into small, thick patties and fry slowly in butter and a little oil. Serve with cranberry sauce. Should you decide to use cooked turkey meat for this, mince it well, then add an egg yolk or two to the mixture to help to hold it together.

Duck Burgers

duck breasts, green onions, plum, honey, soy
sauce, bread crumbs, lettuce, cucumber, chile

Put **2 duck breasts (about 7 ounces / 200g total weight)** into a food
processor, add **a large green onion, a pitted fresh plum, a tablespoon
of honey**, and **a tablespoon of dark soy sauce**. Process to a coarse
mince then add **2½ ounces (75g) fresh white bread crumbs**.

Form the paste into 4 burgers. Roll each in **a few more bread crumbs**,
then fry over low heat for 10 minutes on each side.

Place each burger on **a large, crisp lettuce leaf**, add **shredded
cucumber, chopped green onion**, and **a small, slivered chile**, and
wrap the burgers in the lettuce.

For 3 to 4. Sweet, fruity, and crisp.

A few ideas inspired by the shrimp baguettes

Fish sticks in a sandwich, green herb mayo

Broil or fry fish sticks till crisp. A light cooking should keep them moist inside. Split a baguette in half. Stir some capers, chopped dill, and basil into mayonnaise and spread it over the baguette. Tuck in a lettuce leaf, then the hot, fresh-from-the-pan fish sticks. Squirt with lemon juice. Crisp. Soft. Green. Unapologetic.

Trout in a soft roll

Dust a couple of trout fillets in flour to which you have added a good pinch of smoked paprika. Fry in shallow butter, or oil if you prefer, then drain on paper towels. Sandwich in a soft, fresh roll and squeeze over a little lemon juice.

Shrimp, bacon, wheat toast

Grill a few large shelled shrimp and some bacon. Put them into a sandwich of hot wheat toast spread with a little mango chutney.

Vietnamese Shrimp Baguettes

raw shrimp, cilantro, garlic, chile, lemongrass, fish sauce, rice vinegar, pickled ginger, carrot, ginger, green onion, mayonnaise, toasted sesame oil, baguettes

Put **8 ounces (250g) shelled raw shrimp** in a food processor with **8 cilantro stems, 2 cloves of garlic, a bird's eye chile, a lemongrass stalk, a lump of fresh ginger, 2 teaspoons of Vietnamese fish sauce,** and **2 teaspoons of rice vinegar**. Puree.

Finely shred **half a carrot**. Shred **2 tablespoons Japanese pickled ginger.** Finely slice **a green onion** and toss all three together with **a little fresh cilantro**. Stir **2 teaspoons of toasted sesame oil** into **2 tablespoons of mayonnaise.**

Put the pureed shrimp in a nonstick frying pan and fry, without any oil, for 4 minutes. Toss with the seasoned carrot. Split **2 small baguettes** and spread with the sesame mayo. Stuff with the shrimp hash.

For 2. One of the great sandwiches. IMHO (in my humble opinion).

A few variations on the sausage burgers

Morcilla burger.
Dark blood sausage, white buns

Instead of chorizo, mix 12 ounces (350g) soft morcilla with the pork opposite. Split into 4 and pat into thick burgers. Fry, then stuff into soft, white rolls or sourdough buns.

Choose a softish chorizo rather than one of the harder varieties. It should be only a little firmer than a good fresh sausage.

Pork, juniper.
Breakfast sausage, bright with juniper

Use 1½ pounds (650g) pork sausage meat taken from good, herby breakfast sausages. Grind 6 juniper berries and half a teaspoon of fennel seeds with a pestle and mortar, then stir into the sausage meat. You could include a few herbs, such as oregano, thyme, or ground bay leaf. Shape into 4 thick, flat patties and cook as opposite. Fill the buns with a fennel salad or a tomato and cucumber salsa.

Chorizo Burgers

chorizo, ground pork, ciabatta buns,
salad greens

Remove the skin from **12 ounces (350g) fresh chorizo sausages** and
discard. Put the meat in a mixing bowl, add **8 ounces (250g) ground
pork**, and mix well. The pork will lighten the dense chorizo. The
seasoning will need little, but much depends on your chorizo, some
being more highly flavored than others. Split the mixture into 4 and
roll into balls. Pat each one into a thick patty about 2½ inches (6cm) in
diameter.

Get a nonstick frying pan hot, add **a very thin film of oil**, then place
the burgers in the pan. Let them cook till lightly browned on the
underside, then flip and cook the other side, adjusting the heat
accordingly so they cook through to the middle. Be gentle, or they
may fall apart.

Split **4 ciabatta buns** open, partially fill with **salad greens**, then a
chorizo burger.

For 4. Smoky, succulent.

Good things to put in your summer rolls, served with the dipping sauce opposite

• Coarsely shredded daikon, rice noodles, shelled shrimp, cilantro.
• Shredded red chile, watercress, bean sprouts, sliced roast duck.
• Grilled salmon, cucumber, bok choy, mirin, soy.
• Avocado, tomato, watercress, green onion, mint.

Summer Herb Rolls

cucumber, red chile, carrot, green onion,
rice noodles, spring roll wrappers, mint,
basil, cilantro, chives, ponzu sauce, lime,
rice vinegar, hot chile sauce

Slice **half a cucumber** in half lengthwise, scrape out its seeds with a
teaspoon, then cut the flesh into matchsticks. Very finely slice **a mild,
long red chile**, then cut **a medium-size carrot** into small matchsticks.
Shred **a green onion**.

Pour a kettle of boiling water over **1¾ ounces (50g) rice noodles**
and let them soak for a few minutes. Moisten **2 large spring roll rice
paper wrappers** in warm water, lay them on a work surface, then
divide the shredded vegetables and noodles between them, tucking
6 or 7 basil leaves, 6 or 7 mint leaves, and **6 or 7 cilantro leaves** into
each one as you go. Lay **4 slim chives** onto each one, then wrap the
vegetables up into parcels.

Make a dip for the summer rolls by mixing together **a tablespoon of
ponzu sauce, the juice of half a lime, a teaspoon of rice vinegar**, and
a teaspoon of hot chile sauce. Eat the rolls, cut into two, with the dip.

Makes 2 large rolls. Bright tasting. A hot, refreshing crunch.

Some bagel ideas

Cream cheese, smoked salmon

Thickly cut smoked salmon, generously spread cream cheese, a golden chewy bagel. Bliss. But try adding a few bottled green peppercorns—the sort that come in brine—to the cream cheese; tuck in a slice or 2 of very crisp bacon; stir dill or chives into the cream cheese; toast the bagel on its cut sides, spread thinly with wasabi paste, then add the cream cheese and salmon; or swap the salmon for mackerel.

Chorizo paste

Peel a soft, salami-type (fully cured) chorizo and puree it to a paste in a food processor, adding a little crème fraîche or olive oil to give it a spreadable consistency. Slather generously onto split and toasted bagels.

The Bagel

bagel, mascarpone, balsamic vinegar,
raisins or golden raisins

Put **3 tablespoons of raisins or golden raisins** in a small bowl, pour in
2 tablespoons of balsamic vinegar and **2 tablespoons of warm water**,
and leave the fruit to swell for 20 minutes or so, then drain, reserving
some of the liquid. Split **a bagel** in half horizontally, lightly toast both
cut edges, then brush with some of the soaking liquid from the fruit.

Mix **¾ cup (200g) of mascarpone** with the raisins and spread
thickly over the hot bagel.

For 1. Sweet, warm. Feel-good.

Herb Burgers

kidney beans, butter or flageolet beans, green
onions, garlic, basil, chives, parsley, tomatoes,
rolls, salad greens, mayonnaise

Drain and rinse **a 14-ounce (400g) can of kidney beans** and
a 14-ounce (400g) can of butter or flageolet beans. Finely slice **6 green
onions** and let them soften in **a tablespoon of oil** over moderate
heat. Don't let them brown. Peel and crush **2 cloves of garlic** and add
them together with **a large handful of basil leaves, 8 finely chopped
chives,** and **a handful of parsley,** chopped. Add the beans and season.

Using a potato masher, partially crush the mixture so there is a
combination of smooth and rough, producing a texture that will be
interesting to eat. Mold small balls of the mixture into thick, flat patties.
You will get about 12. They are fragile, so treat them carefully, setting
them down on a baking sheet, then refrigerate for a good 20 minutes.

Warm **a thin layer of oil** in a nonstick frying pan, then place the patties
down in the pan, a few at time, leaving room to flip them over. When
the underside is golden brown, carefully turn the patties over and cook
the other side. Drain briefly on paper towels before stuffing them into
toasted rolls with **slices of tomato, salad greens,** and **a slather of
mayonnaise.** For 6.

Tomato Caesar Bruschetta

tomatoes, Little Gem lettuce, ciabatta,
garlic, egg yolk, vinegar, Dijon mustard

Slice **14 ounces (400g) tomatoes** in half and place them, cut side up, on a stove-top grill pan or baking sheet. Cut **2 Little Gem lettuces** in half and tuck them in among the tomatoes. Season, drizzle with **a little oil**, then broil or grill for a few minutes, till the lettuce has just started to color and the tomatoes are soft.

Make the dressing. Peel **2 garlic cloves** and drop them into a blender. Add **an egg yolk, a tablespoon of white wine vinegar, a tablespoon of Dijon mustard**, then **4 tablespoons of olive oil**. Blend till smooth and thick. (You can also do this by hand, in the way you would make mayonnaise, beating the oil into the other ingredients with a balloon whisk.) Check the seasoning.

Split **a large ciabatta loaf** and toast it on the cut sides. Place toasted side up on a cutting board, drizzle with a generous amount of olive oil, then cover with the tomatoes and lettuce. Spoon over the dressing and eat immediately, while the tomatoes are still hot and the bread is crisp.

For 4. Crisp, sweet, luscious.

A few ideas for beef

Steak sandwich, buttery greens

Heat a well-seasoned or nonstick frying pan over moderate heat, add a salted and peppered rib-eye steak, and let it brown for a couple of minutes, without any oil or fat. Turn and cook the other side, then turn it again a couple of times. Slide a thick slice of butter under the steak—it will melt immediately—and let the meat soak some of it up, then turn it over in the butter, keeping the heat at a temperature that will not let it burn. Remove the steak and let it rest for a good 5 minutes. Melt a little more butter in the pan, add a few thinly shredded spring greens, and fry till soft and bright. Split open a baguette, slice the steak into thick strips, and stuff into the bread with the hot, buttery greens.

And a messy beef hash

Coarsely grate a potato, skin on, then fry it in a little beef dripping with a finely sliced onion until it colors. Add some chopped parsley and thyme. Pour in some of the beef juices from the roast, then add the crisp ends of the roast, bits of golden fat, and any interesting crusty bits left behind after the roast has been removed from the pan. When all is sizzling, pile the mixture onto rolls.

A Beef Sandwich

leftover gravy, cherry tomatoes, roast beef
leftovers, fresh horseradish, mayonnaise, rolls

Warm **the roasting juices and gravy from Sunday's roast beef** over
moderate heat, including any bits left in the pan. When they start to
bubble, add **a handful of cherry tomatoes**, cut in half, and let them
cook till they color lightly. Crush the tomatoes in the gravy with a fork.

Finely grate **a little fresh horseradish** and stir it into some
mayonnaise. Cut **rolls** in half lengthwise, spread them generously
with the horseradish mayonnaise, and fill them with **slices of beef**
cut from the cold roast. Put dishes of the hot gravy on the table and
dip the rolls in as you eat.

Other ideas for a meatless sandwich

Mozzarella and basil

Split a small ciabatta down its length. Toast the cut sides lightly and spread with basil pesto. Cover with slices of buffalo mozzarella, then stir a little more olive oil into the pesto and trickle it over the cheese. Grill till the cheese melts, but stop before it colors.

Onion, quince paste, and blue cheese

Thinly slice a large onion, fry it in a little butter till nutty golden brown, then stir in a tablespoon or two of quince paste. When it bubbles, pile the mixture onto sourdough bread and cover with slices of blue cheese such as Picos, Cabrales, or Stichelton.

Labne and mint in pita

Warm some pita bread in the oven or under a broiler, split it, then stuff with labne or feta (crumbled in a little yogurt with dried oregano), plus some mint leaves and a good, thick, sweet olive oil.

Soft cheese, anchovy paste

Spread thin slices of sourdough bread with anchovy paste. Cover with slices of Camembert, Waterloo, or similar semisoft cheese, then add a second slice of anchovy-spread bread on top. Cook using a panini press, or place in a frying pan in a little quietly sizzling butter and oil, pressing the sandwich down on both sides till it browns.

Bresaola, Emmentaler, and Pickled Cucumber Sandwich

sourdough bread, bresaola, Emmentaler cheese, sugar, cucumber, white wine vinegar, Dijon mustard

Lightly peel **half a cucumber** with a vegetable peeler, then halve it down its length and scrape out and discard the seeds. Peel into long, pappardelle-like strips. Put **3 tablespoons of white wine vinegar, 1 tablespoon of Dijon mustard, a teaspoon of sugar**, and a little pepper into a mixing bowl and add the cucumber. Leave for 10 minutes.

To make the sandwich, fry **4 very thin slices of sourdough bread** in **butter** till lightly crisp on both sides, then drain on paper towels. Pile 2 slices with **thinly sliced Emmentaler cheese**, strips of the pickled cucumber, a little salt, and **some thin slices of bresaola**. Then add the final slices of bread.

For 2. Toothsome.

A couple more ideas for a chicken sandwich

With bacon and chile-cilantro mayo

Cook a few slices of bacon till truly crisp. Finely chop a small chile, removing the seeds as you go. Fry in a little oil, then stir into 4 or 5 tablespoons of mayonnaise together with a handful of finely chopped cilantro leaves. Pull some cold roast chicken to shreds and fold into the chile-cilantro mayo. Pile the mixture onto rolls, tucking the crisp bacon in as you go.

Herb mayonnaise, radish, cucumber

Peel, seed, and dice some cucumber. Trim a few radishes and slice them in half lengthwise. Add to the herb mayonnaise opposite with some coarsely torn pieces of roast chicken. Pile onto dark rye bread, preferably in a curl of perfect, crisp summer lettuce.

Chicken, Asparagus, and Avocado Sandwich

cold roast chicken, basil, tarragon, dill, mayonnaise, asparagus, avocado, lettuce, green onions, sourdough bread

Boil **8 small asparagus spears** in a pot of water till just tender (they should still be slightly crisp for this), then drain. Slice them in half lengthwise and set aside. Shred **2 crisp iceberg lettuce leaves**. Trim **4 green onions** and halve lengthwise. Peel and slice **a small avocado**. Slice **a cooked chicken breast**, or remove slices from yesterday's Sunday roast.

Put **4 heaping tablespoons of mayonnaise** in a bowl, stir in **a tablespoon each of chopped basil, tarragon**, and **dill**, and season lightly with salt. Toast **4 slices of sourdough bread** and spread each of them with the herb mayonnaise. Top 2 of the slices with the lettuce and asparagus spears, followed by the green onions and avocado. Place slices of chicken on top and sandwich together with the remaining bread.

Makes 2 heavily laden sandwiches. Toasted sourdough, herb mayo, cold chicken, ice-cold lettuce, and avocado. Possibly my favorite sandwich.

A few variations on the sausage sandwich

Sweet onions

Fry or broil a seriously good pork sausage. Peel and thinly slice a couple of onions and let them cook in a little butter till truly soft. Add a splash of balsamic or sherry vinegar. Add to the sausage as you stuff it into a roll.

Sausage and cheese

Fry or broil a pork sausage or two. Slice in half and place cut side up on a broiler pan. Place a slice of cheese—fontina, Comté, or other firm variety—on top and broil till it melts. Slide into a roll.

Mozzarella Chorizo Sandwich

mozzarella, chorizo, ciabatta, spinach

Slice **4½ ounces (130g) fresh chorizo** thickly on the diagonal, then place the slices in a large, heavy frying pan over medium heat. There is no need to use any oil or butter. Cook gently for 4 to 5 minutes, turning halfway through, until the oil begins to escape from the sausage.

Slice **a large ball of mozzarella (about 5 ounces / 150g)** on top of the chorizo, then carefully spoon some of the oil from the pan over the top. Cook for 2 to 3 minutes to allow the cheese to melt—covering with a lid will help—then season with a few twists of freshly ground black pepper.

Tear open **a short ciabatta**, spoon the chorizo and mozzarella inside, then spoon the juices from the pan over the top. Again, there is no need to butter the bread. The pan juices will ensure it gets deliciously moist.

Tuck **a handful of spinach leaves** inside the ciabatta. Give it a good squeeze, allowing all the juices to soak into the bread and the spinach to wilt a little. Slice the ciabatta in half and serve immediately.

For 2. It's all about the juices.

Some ideas for ham sandwiches

The French

If the bread and ham are of the best quality, then a ham sandwich needs nothing more than a spread of mustard. A perfect baguette, thin, hand-cut ham, a dab of mustard. That is all. If only life was always as simple as this.

The English

There are two sorts of British ham sandwich: the thin, triangular afternoon-tea sandwich, which I am not concerned with here, and the chunkier, more satisfying version. The English farmhouse ham sandwich probably needs thick, impeccably fresh bread, coarsely torn ham, and a thick layer of mustard. Embellish as you think fit, with lettuce, mayonnaise, tomato, or whatever else takes your fancy.

Panini

The delightful little ciabatta-style stuffed bread. Rectangular, shallow, light. The bread is chewy, the filling can be pretty much anything you fancy, but mozzarella often features and crisp, bright green lettuce is pretty much compulsory, as are slices of tomato.

Ham and cheese works. Always has. But try:

- A smear of wasabi on your ham sandwich.
- A brush of green olive paste is worth pursuing.
- Watercress, arugula, basil—peppery things—always cheer up a ham roll.
- A spoonful of creamy scrambled egg makes a substantial twist.
- Warm some thickly sliced jarred artichokes in olive oil and toss them with the ham.
- Brush baby leeks or green onions with olive oil and grill till soft. Sprinkle with grated Parmesan cheese. Grill once again till the cheese is golden, then pile on top of the ham.
- Fry slices of prosciutto briefly till they curl and crisp, then pile them onto soft white bread.

Pork Rillettes, Gherkins, and Onion Sourdough

pork rillettes, gherkins, green
onion, sourdough bread

Put **a large green onion** (2 or 3 if small) in a food processor with
5 tablespoons of olive oil, add some salt and pepper, then puree to a
green paste. Soak **4 slices of sourdough bread** in this green onion oil.

Fry the bread in a nonstick pan till very crisp on both sides. Drain
briefly on paper towels, then spread 2 slices with **2 tablespoons of
pork rillettes** and add **a few gherkin slices**. Top on. Drizzle on the last
bit of green onion marinade. Eat.

Makes 2 sandwiches. Sweet-sharp and crisp.

A couple of variations on the chicken baguette

A sort of teriyaki sandwich

Mix together 3½ tablespoons (50ml) peanut oil, 3½ tablespoons (50ml) soy sauce, a crushed clove of garlic, 2 tablespoons of mirin, a pinch of sugar, and a pinch of red pepper flakes. Let 2 salmon steaks soak in it for 20 minutes, turning occasionally, then broil till crisp and dark on the outside. Break into large pieces, then stuff into split baguettes with slices of cucumber and soft green leaves such as mâche.

Chile-spiced chicken rolls

Cut 14 ounces (400g) chicken meat into thin strips. In a food processor process a medium-hot seeded chile, a pinch of red pepper flakes, 2 cloves of garlic, a small handful of mint leaves, the juice of a large lemon, and 4 tablespoons of oil to a coarse paste. Toss the meat in the spice mixture and set aside for 20 minutes. Grill the chicken and any clinging marinade till sizzling (there will be quite a bit of smoke), then stuff the hot, spicy chicken into rolls, with watercress or crisp lettuce.

Stir-Fried Chicken Baguette

chicken breast, bean sprouts, lemongrass, cilantro, mint, chiles, ginger, toasted sesame oil, mayonnaise, soy sauce, baguette

In a food processor, puree the following: **a lemongrass stalk, 2 red bird's eye chiles, a peeled walnut-size piece of fresh ginger, a handful of cilantro, a bunch of mint**, and **a little toasted sesame oil**.

Remove the skin from **a chicken breast**, then slice into six. Fry in a wok with **a little oil** till golden. Add the spice paste, let it sizzle, then throw in **a handful of bean sprouts**. Season **mayonnaise** with **a little soy sauce**. Split **pieces of baguette** lengthwise, spread with the mayonnaise, then stuff with the chicken and bean sprout mixture.

For 2. Fiery, with the refreshing crunch of bean sprout and mint.

Fig and Goat Cheese Focaccia

figs, goat cheese, honey, focaccia, rosemary

Split **a piece of focaccia,** about 4 x 6 inches (10 x 15cm), horizontally to give two rectangles, then place them side by side in a shallow dish or baking sheet. Preheat the oven to 400°F (200°C).

Pour **4 tablespoons of honey** over the focaccia (if you are using thick honey, then warm the jar first in a small pan of boiling water to make it runny). Slice **5 figs** into four from top to bottom and place over the focaccia, then trickle over **another tablespoon of honey** and **a few finely chopped rosemary leaves**. Bake for 15 minutes. Remove and turn the oven to the broil setting.

Slice **3½ ounces (100g) goat cheese** into thick rounds and place on top of the figs. Broil for 5 minutes, until the cheese starts to melt. Serve immediately.

For 2. Crisp bread. Melting cheese. Sweet figs.

More ideas for burgers

Jerk burger

Season the burger opposite with purchased jerk seasoning—the best of them contain allspice, cloves, cinnamon, thyme, and chile. Fry the burgers, then serve in soft toasted buns with a little cooked spinach, or, if you are near a West Indian market, try and get hold of some callaloo.

Gorgonzola, the richest burger

Instead of the ricotta, double up on the beef. Place each burger in your hand and press a ball of Gorgonzola into the center, then squeeze the meat around it so it covers the cheese. Carefully flatten out into a thick patty, then fry as opposite. Soft toasted buns and slices of ripe tomato complete them.

A burger with attitude

Chop a gherkin. Not finely. Not coarsely. Add it to the beef. Stir in a sprinkling of sesame seeds, a little ketchup, salt and pepper, and some hot French mustard. Shape and fry.

Ricotta Burgers

ground beef, ricotta, green onions, capers, rosemary, sun-dried tomatoes, sherry vinegar, ciabatta

Mix together **14 ounces (400g) ground beef, 7 ounces (200g) ricotta, 4 chopped green onions, 1 tablespoon of capers**, and **a bit of chopped fresh rosemary**. Season well with salt and freshly ground black pepper.

Shape the mixture into 6 thick burgers, about 2½ inches (6cm) in diameter, then leave for as long as you can in the fridge to firm up. Fry the burgers in **a little olive oil** in a shallow nonstick pan for 6 to 8 minutes per side.

For the relish, chop **a scant cup (100g) sun-dried tomatoes** (the sort that come in oil) and mix with a little of the oil from the jar. Add **a tablespoon of sherry vinegar** and season with salt and pepper. When the patties are cooked, sandwich them between **6 ciabatta rolls** spread with the relish.

For 6. A fresh take on the classic burger.

Tomato Focaccia

tomatoes, focaccia, ricotta, basil, olive oil

Make a basil oil by processing **10 basil leaves** and **5 tablespoons of olive oil** in a blender or food processor till you have a bright green dressing. Slice **a couple of large tomatoes** in half and broil till soft and slightly charred at the edges.

Split **a rectangle of focaccia**, about 4 inches (10cm) long, horizontally and brush with some of the basil oil. Broil till lightly crisp. Spread **a generous tablespoon of ricotta** on top, then add the tomatoes and drizzle any spare dressing on top.

For 1. High-summer lunch.

A few ideas for pork sandwiches

The pork crackling sandwich

Thin slices of roast pork, shredded crackling, a smear of applesauce. Roast pork, cut ⅛ inch (3mm) thick. A russet apple, sliced but not peeled. Gravy. Whole wheat bread, untoasted.

The pork rib sandwich

Slice the meat from last night's barbecued ribs. You will probably get in a sticky mess. Cut the meat into thin shreds, then stir into mayonnaise together with a couple of tablespoons of the barbecue sauce, tasting as you go. Pile a piece of soft, good bread—ciabatta or a bun—with a little shredded carrot or some chopped apple and some tufts of watercress, then pile on top of the pork.

A rare delight (let's face it, it's not that often you have leftover barbecued ribs), but one of the most memorable sandwiches I have ever eaten and one I felt I should share.

Apple pork roll

Finely chop a sweet apple, removing the core as you go. Warm the juices, fat, and interesting bits from the roasting pan, then stir in the chopped apple, a dash of cider if needs be, or perhaps a little Marsala. Briefly add thinly sliced cold pork, then stuff into a roll, letting the juices soak through the bread. Glorious.

The Sunday Roast
Pork Sandwich

leftover roast pork, roast potatoes, crackling
and roasting juices, bread, applesauce

Slice the **leftover pork** very finely and salt it generously. Cut up the
leftover **roast potatoes** and warm them in the **juices** from the roasting
pan. Spread the **bread**—a sandwich roll would be spot-on too—with
applesauce or mayonnaise. Add the hot roast potatoes, the slices of
pork, a bit of **crackling** if you have it, and then spoon over the warm
roasting juices.

In a bowl

There is much pleasure to be found in a bowl of soup. Cradling our food is a great comfort, especially when it comes in the form of an aromatic liquid such as a steaming broth or thick soup. This is food that instantly soothes and satiates, warms and satisfies. Food that restores.

There is something right about food in a bowl. The hot liquid on your spoon; the warmth of the bowl in your hands; the final scraping of spoon against china—they enable us to feel closer to what we eat. Unlike a plate on a table, a bowl allows us to feel the heat of our food through the porcelain.

The shape of a bowl traps the smell of our food, like a wineglass. As we hold it in our hands and dip in our spoon, fork, or chopsticks, we experience more of its fragrance: the scent of sweet garlic, warm rice, hot milk, deep broth. Of course we can't cut food that's in a bowl, and neither should we. The ingredients should be in small enough pieces that no knife is required.

Meals in a bowl are probably at their best when they are simple. I have always loved rice in a bowl. Just plain, white rice. Pure and unsullied. You know you could, if necessary, survive on it. You feel you need nothing more.

But there is more. Oh glory, yes. A little stew of chicken with herbs; a deep, salty broth of beef stock and green vegetables; a spicy *laksa*; a dal thick with soft lentils and spice; a Vietnamese-style *pho* with slithery noodles and cilantro. The simplicity of a bowl of golden chicken stock.

Our bowl can be as simple or as elaborate as we wish. A crude earthenware container, a delicate porcelain receptacle, a workaday white soup dish, a piece of ironmonger's enamel, something hand thrown, a family heirloom, or something disposable. Whatever we use, it fulfills the same purpose. To hold our food and enable us, should we wish, to cradle it. Comfort food at its most satisfying.

A few favorites

A simple miso broth for a fragile moment

Bring 4 cups (1 liter) of chicken or vegetable stock or dashi almost to a boil (powdered dashi works well here). Stir in 3 tablespoons of light miso, a tablespoon of toasted sesame oil, and a couple of tablespoons of soy sauce. Simmer for 3 or 4 minutes, then turn off the heat. To this you can add thinly sliced cabbage or kale, plus paper-fine slices of radish, carrot, or fried mushrooms. I like to put cilantro in mine, too.

Yellow split peas, spices, and tomato

A rich, thick dal in just over half an hour. Boil 8 ounces (250g) yellow split peas in 4 cups (1 liter) of water for about 35 minutes, till almost soft, then drain. In a saucepan, lightly brown a sliced onion in a little oil, then add 2 teaspoons of cumin seeds, a 1-inch (2.5cm) piece of ginger, peeled and shredded into fine matchsticks, and 2 cloves of crushed garlic. Stir in a teaspoon of ground turmeric and a pinch of red pepper flakes, then add a 14-ounce (400g) can of chopped tomatoes. Stir in the cooked split peas. Keep cooking for 10 to 15 minutes, adding vegetable stock or boiling water if necessary, and crushing some of the peas as you stir (or use a vegetable masher). Finish with a teaspoon of garam masala, salt, and some fresh cilantro. Eat with warm Indian bread or rice. For 4.

A light, fresh, sweet soup for summer

Separate the leaves of a head of soft, large-leaved lettuce. Melt a thick slice of butter in a deep pan, add a large, finely chopped shallot, and let it soften. Add the lettuce, coarsely torn, then stir in 2¾ cups (400g) shelled peas. Simmer for 10 minutes, then puree in a blender or food processor in small batches.

The deep savor of beef and noodle broth

Mix together a tablespoon of oyster sauce, a tablespoon of fish sauce, a teaspoon of toasted sesame oil, and 2 teaspoons of honey. Brush this over sirloin steak and broil or cook on the stove top, leaving the outside with a dark crust, the inside generously pink. Bring 4 cups (1 liter) of beef stock to a boil. Pour boiling water over 3½ ounces (100g) rice noodles and let them hydrate, about 2 minutes, then drain and place in serving bowls. Slice the steak thickly and place on top of the noodles; scatter with sliced green onions, chopped cilantro, a handful of watercress, and a little finely chopped red chile. Ladle over the broth. Season with lime juice. For 2.

Carrot, Black Beans, and Cilantro

carrots, butter, black beans, cilantro leaves,
mustard seeds, onion, red pepper flakes

Boil **1¼ pounds (600g) carrots** in a large pot of lightly salted water until tender, then drain, reserving the liquid. Puree the carrots in a food processor with **1½ tablespoons (20g) butter** and ⅔ cup (150ml) of the reserved cooking water.

Melt **2 tablespoons (30g) butter** in a shallow pan, add **2 teaspoons of mustard seeds**, and toast for a minute or two. Drain **two 14-ounce (400g) cans of black beans**, add to the pan, cover, and leave to cook for 5 minutes, till warmed through.

Peel and finely slice **an onion**. Melt another **2 tablespoons (30g) butter** in a pan, add the sliced onion, and fry till golden brown. Scatter in **a large pinch of red pepper flakes** and a further **teaspoon of mustard seeds**. Sizzle briefly.

Divide the carrot puree between 2 bowls, gently stir in the black beans, scatter over **a few cilantro leaves**, then spoon over the sizzling onion and its butter.

For 2. Aromatic, satisfying, sweet, and faintly hot.

Split Peas with Eggplant

yellow split peas, eggplant, onion, cardamom
pods, turmeric, cumin seeds, canned tomatoes,
cilantro leaves

Soak **3½ ounces (100g) yellow split peas** for an hour, or longer if
you have it. Peel and coarsely chop **an onion**, then let it soften in
a little oil in a deep pan over moderate heat. Crack open **10 green
cardamom pods**, extract their tiny black seeds, and lightly grind them
with a pestle and mortar or in a spice grinder. Stir **a teaspoon of
cumin seeds** into the onion, then add the cardamom seeds. When all
is golden and fragrant, add **2 teaspoons of ground turmeric**. Stir in
a 14-ounce (400g) can of chopped tomatoes and continue to simmer.

   In a separate pan, boil the yellow split peas in deep unsalted water
for about 30 minutes, till soft. Drain and stir into the onion and
tomato mixture. Simmer, stirring regularly, till soft, scarlet, and
slushy, then season with salt and pepper. Halve and thinly slice
an eggplant, then cook in **several tablespoons of olive oil** in a
shallow pan till soft and golden. Drain and stir into the split peas,
adding **a handful of cilantro leaves**. Serve with steamed white rice.

   For 2. Rich and earthy. Glowing colors.

Green Vegetable Soup

spring vegetables, white peppercorns, coriander
seeds, turmeric, lemongrass, garlic, ginger,
chile, cilantro, vegetable stock, coconut milk,
fish sauce, lime, soy sauce

Put **a teaspoon of white peppercorns** and **a teaspoon of coriander seeds** in a dry nonstick frying pan and toast lightly for 2 or 3 minutes, then tip into the bowl of a food processor. Add **a half teaspoon of sea salt, a teaspoon of ground turmeric, 2 chopped lemongrass stalks, 2 cloves peeled garlic, a 1¼-inch (3cm) lump of peeled ginger, 3 hot green chiles, 3 tablespoons of peanut oil**, and **a handful of cilantro stems and roots**. Puree to a coarse paste. You can keep this paste for a few days in the fridge, its surface covered with oil to prevent it from drying out.

In a deep pan, fry **3 lightly heaping tablespoons of the curry paste** in **a tablespoon of oil** for 30 seconds, till fragrant, stirring as you go. Stir in **¾ cup (200ml) vegetable stock** and **1 cup (250ml) coconut milk, a tablespoon of fish sauce**, and **2 tablespoons of lime juice**.

Add a **1-pound (450g) mixture of asparagus tips, fava beans**, and **peas** and continue simmering for 5 to 6 minutes, then shred **a couple of handfuls of greens** into thick ribbons and add them to the pan.

Finish the soup with **a pinch of sugar, fish sauce, a little soy sauce, more lime juice**—whatever floats your boat.

For 4. Deep flavors that dazzle. Rich but fresh.

Quiet, old-fashioned flavors for leftover ham hock

Make a crisp, light salad using Belgian endive and inner lettuce leaves tossed with generous handfuls of coarsely chopped mint, parsley, and basil. Dress with a finely chopped shallot, lemon juice, salt, and olive oil. Tear rough chunks of ham from the bone and toss with the dressed leaves. Serve with halved hard-boiled eggs, still quite soft in the middle.

Ham Hock, Herb Sauce

ham hock, peas, garlic, parsley, chives, basil

Put a **1- to 1¼-pound (500 to 600g) ham hock** in a deep pan with just enough water to cover. Bring to a boil, skim off the froth that rises to the surface, then turn the heat down so the liquid simmers. Cover with a lid and leave, with the occasional turn, for 45 to 50 minutes or so, till the ham is cooked through to the bone.

Remove the ham from the cooking liquid, add **1⅓ cups (200g) fresh or frozen shelled peas**, and **a large clove of garlic** and cook for 5 minutes or so, till the peas are tender. Add **a handful of parsley, a handful of chives**, and **a handful of basil leaves** to the peas, cook a minute or so longer, then puree in a blender to give a thick, green sauce. Add pepper if necessary.

Tear the ham from its bone in large pieces. Coarsely chop **a few more of the herbs**, then roll the pieces of ham in them. Spoon the sauce into bowls and add the pieces of ham.

For 2. The nannying quality of peas and ham, the vitality of fresh herbs.

A few thoughts on the shrimp soup

You could add some cooked noodles if you feel like it, or small pea eggplants that have been halved and lightly fried, or some Thai basil leaves, or fish instead of the shrimp.

For a change

Greens and bean sprouts. The warmth of coconut and noodles

Put the spice paste opposite into a deep pan, sauté briefly, then stir in 1 cup (250ml) each coconut milk and chicken stock and bring to a boil. Soak 7 ounces (200g) rice noodles in boiling water, drain, and divide among 4 bowls. Add a handful of Chinese broccoli or bok choy to the stock. Once it softens, add a handful of bean sprouts and a sliced green onion, then divide among the bowls, ladling it over the noodles. For 4.

Shrimp, crisp lettuce, and miso. Light, fresh, satisfying.

Whisk together 3 tablespoons of white (shiro) miso and 3 cups (750ml) vegetable stock and bring to a boil. Turn the heat down to a simmer and stir in 2 teaspoons each of soy sauce and hot chile sauce. Shred a couple of crisp white lettuce leaves and their stems and put them in 2 deep soup bowls. Add a finely sliced green onion and a large handful of cooked shrimp to each bowl, then a handful of cilantro leaves. Ladle the hot soup over the lettuce and shrimp.

Shrimp, Lemongrass, and Coconut

shrimp, lemongrass, coconut milk, cilantro, turmeric, garlic, bird's eye chiles, galangal or ginger, bok choy, mirin, fish sauce, lime, mint

Put **6 cilantro stalks and roots, 2 teaspoons of ground turmeric, 2 large garlic cloves, 2 lemongrass stalks, 2 bird's eye chiles, 2 tablespoons of peanut oil**, and **a thumb-size knob of peeled galangal or ginger** in a food processor and reduce to a rough, loose paste. (This will make twice as much as you need.)

Put half the paste in a pan, fry for a couple of minutes, stirring regularly, then add **a 14-ounce (400ml) can of coconut milk, a head of bok choy**, cut into large bite-size pieces, and **8 to 10 large, raw shelled shrimp**. Bring to a boil and simmer for a few minutes, till the shrimp turn opaque. Finish with **2 teaspoons of mirin, a tablespoon of fish sauce**, and **the juice of a lime**, or to taste. Stir in **the leaves from the cilantro** and top with **a few mint leaves**.

For 2. Vivid flavors, a little heat. Uplifting and energizing.

Rib and Rhubarb Broth

small pork ribs, rhubarb, chicken stock, star
anise, peppercorns, bay leaves, green onions

In a large, deep pan, brown **1 pound (500g) small pork ribs** on both
sides in **a little oil**. When they are nicely colored, pour over **4 cups
(1 liter) of chicken stock**, add **2 star anise, 8 peppercorns**, and
a couple of bay leaves, and bring to a boil. Lower the heat so the liquid
continues cooking at a low simmer and leave for 50 minutes to an
hour, keeping an eye on the liquid so it doesn't boil away; you want to
end up with a rich, quite concentrated broth. Check the seasoning.

Remove the ribs from the liquid, pull the meat from the bones, and
cut it into chunks (sometimes I leave them whole). Coarsely chop
2 green onions and drop them, together with the meat, into the hot
broth. Pour into bowls. Thinly slice **a small stalk of rhubarb** (you may
not need all of it) into long matchsticks and add a few pieces to each
bowl of broth. Serve immediately, just as the rhubarb starts to soften.

For 4. Savory depth, sharp fruit.

A few thoughts on the chicken broth

I often make a chicken broth with the bones from the Sunday roast. The trick is to remember to add all the jelly and bits of savory goodness that lie under the roasted bird. A 20-minute simmer with a small halved onion, a few black peppercorns, a tomato, and a few parsley sprigs will produce a golden-brown broth with deep flavor. The other thing worth considering is the ready-made stocks in the refrigerated case at the supermarket or butcher's shop. Expensive but often very good indeed.

Other variations

Chicken wing onion broth

Slice 2 large green onions and cut lengthwise through the bulbs (chop the green part). Brown them in a little oil in a wide pan. Add 12 small shallots, peeled but left whole, brown them gently, then remove the green onions and shallots from the pan. Add 6 seasoned chicken wings and brown on all sides. Add 4 cups (1 liter) of chicken stock, return the green onions and shallots to the pan, and simmer for 5 to 10 minutes. Add 3½ ounces (100g) noodles and simmer for a few minutes. Season thoughtfully with salt and pepper. Makes 2 deep bowls.

Grilled chicken miso broth

Mix together a teaspoon of fish sauce, a teaspoon of mirin, and a tablespoon of hoisin sauce. Brush this over 2 boneless chicken breasts, then cook under a broiler till the chicken is cooked through to the center. Steam or boil 6 stalks of thin-stemmed broccoli, then refresh under cold running water to keep them green. Heat 3 cups (750ml) good chicken stock in a saucepan, then whisk in a tablespoon of white (shiro) miso paste and a small lump of ginger, peeled and shredded. Slice each chicken breast into 6 pieces and place in 2 large, shallow bowls. Add a little chopped mint and cilantro and the cooked broccoli, then ladle the hot miso chicken broth over the top.

Chicken, Asparagus, and Noodle Broth

chicken thighs, asparagus, noodles,
mushrooms, garlic, chicken stock

Brown **4 chicken thighs** in **a little oil** in a deep pan. Slice **5 ounces (150g) mushrooms, such as large portobello or porcini,** and peel and slice **2 garlic cloves**. Add the mushrooms and garlic to the pan and continue browning, adding more oil if necessary. Pour in **4 cups (1 liter) of chicken stock**, bring to a boil, and simmer for about 30 minutes. Lift out the thighs and take the meat off the bones, returning it to the simmering stock. Shave **4 asparagus spears** into ribbons with a vegetable peeler, then add them to the soup with **7 ounces (200g) noodles**. Cook for a minute or two, then ladle into deep bowls.

For 2 to 3. Big, generous bowls of noodles. Rich chicken broth. The sweetness of asparagus.

To enjoy with the mash

Carrot mash makes a sweet and light accompaniment to any lamb
dish but especially lamb chops that have been grilled with rosemary,
steaks fried with thyme and garlic, and any lamb stew where there
are savory juices to work into the carrot mash with your fork.

Carrot and Bulgur Porridge

carrots, bulgur wheat, vegetable stock, mustard, cilantro, butter

Coarsely chop **1 pound (500g) winter carrots** and cook them in **4 cups (1 liter) of vegetable stock** till tender. Puree them, together with the stock, in a blender or food processor, then return to the pan over moderate heat. Add **1¼ cups (200g) bulgur wheat** and simmer, stirring, for 10 to 15 minutes, until the wheat is tender. Season with salt, pepper, and **a heaping tablespoon of whole-grain mustard**, then finish with **a handful of cilantro leaves** and about **3 tablespoons (40g) butter**.

For 4. Somewhere between soup and pilaf. Soothing, frugal food for a rainy night.

Another idea from the soup

Butter, short-grain rice, some of the soup opposite, a handful of parsley

Put the soup on to warm. Melt 2½ tablespoons (35g) butter in a pan. Add 1 cup (200g) arborio rice, then slowly stir in the hot soup, bit by bit, as if you were adding stock to a risotto, simmering and stirring for 20 minutes or so. Add extra vegetable stock if it appears to be getting too thick, but keep stirring regularly till the rice is al dente.

Remove the flesh from the 2 reserved cooked thighs and add to the risotto. Stir in 3 heaping tablespoons of freshly chopped parsley.

Jerusalem Artichoke and Chicken Soup

Jerusalem artichokes, chicken, onions, butter

Lightly brown **6 bone-in chicken thighs** in **a little olive or peanut oil** and remove. Peel and coarsely chop **1½ pounds (700g) Jerusalem artichokes** and **2 onions**. Put them both in the chicken pan with a little oil. Fry for 7 to 10 minutes, till lightly golden, then return the chicken to the pan, add enough water to cover, bring to a boil, and simmer for 30 minutes.

Remove the chicken, reserve 2 thighs for the risotto tomorrow, then slice the meat from the bones of the remaining thighs. Puree the soup in a food processor or blender until smooth. Check the seasoning, then add **2 tablespoons (25g) butter**, stir, and pour into bowls. Add the chicken to the bowls.

For 2. Soothing soup for today, risotto for tomorrow.

Roast Chicken Pho

chicken thighs, rice noodles, dark soy sauce,
honey, fish sauce, mirin, ginger, lime juice,
star anise, chicken stock, chile, greens

Mix **a tablespoon of dark soy sauce** with **a tablespoon of honey,
a tablespoon each of fish sauce** and **mirin**, and **a chopped red chile.**
Pour into a small roasting pan, add **4 chicken thighs**, and turn them
over in the mixture till lightly coated. Roast in an oven heated to 400°F
(200°C) for about 25 to 30 minutes, occasionally turning the thighs over
in the honey and mirin. They should be very dark and sticky.

In a saucepan, heat **3⅓ cups (800ml) chicken stock** with **6 coin-size
slices of fresh ginger, 2 tablespoons of lime juice**, and **3 star anise.**
As it approaches a boil, add **a small handful of shredded greens or
chard**, leaving them to cook for only a minute or two.

Put **3½ ounces (100g) wide rice noodles** in a heatproof bowl and
cover with boiling water. Leave them to soak for a couple of minutes
until they are soft and silky.

Drain the noodles and divide between 2 deep bowls, slice the
chicken from its bones, and add to the noodles together with the
greens, then ladle the stock on top.

For 2. Healing broth. Sweet roasted chicken.

For a change from the fish soup

Haddock and cod are also suitable candidates for a spiced fish soup.

Rust-colored, lightly spiced broth, firm white fish

Thickly slice 3½ ounces (100g) salami-type (fully cured) chorizo
and cut the slices into thick strips. Cook them in a deep pan over
moderate heat till the oil starts to run and the pieces are sizzling
gently. Add a crushed garlic clove and a finely chopped small onion
and fry till soft. Stir in a teaspoon or so of chopped rosemary. Add
¾ cup (200ml) tomato puree and 1½ cups (350ml) vegetable stock and
bring to a boil. Add 14 ounces (400g) hake, haddock, or cod, cut into
large pieces, and cook for 4 or 5 minutes, till the fish is opaque. Add
a handful of chopped parsley, correct the seasoning, and serve.

Sour, hot, refreshing. A quick crawfish soup

Sauté 2 tablespoons of green curry paste in a little oil, then pour in
3⅓ cups (800ml) vegetable stock. Add 4 crumbled kaffir lime leaves
or 2 well-bashed stalks of lemongrass and a couple of coins of sliced
fresh ginger. Simmer for 10 minutes, then add 2 diced tomatoes,
10 ounces (300g) prepared crawfish tails, and a shot of lime juice. As
the shellfish warms through, add a handful of torn cilantro leaves
and a splash of fish sauce.

Spiced Fish Soup

mussels, pollack fillet, mustard seeds,
chile powder, turmeric, shallots,
cherry tomatoes, cilantro

Clean **2 pounds (1kg) mussels**, discarding any with cracked or broken shells and any open ones that refuse to close when tapped on the side of the kitchen sink. Tug off any wiry beards. Put the mussels in a large, deep pan with **2 cups (500ml) water** and bring to a boil. When the shells open, remove the mussels, reserving the liquid, and take them out of their shells. Discard any that don't open. Strain the liquid through a fine-mesh sieve.

Peel **2 large shallots** and separate the layers, then cook them in **a little oil** in a shallow pan until softened. Add **a tablespoon of mustard seeds, half a teaspoon of chile powder**, and **2 teaspoons of turmeric** and cook for 3 to 4 minutes. Halve **12 cherry tomatoes** and add to the shallots and spices, letting them soften over moderate heat for 5 minutes or so. Pour in the reserved mussel stock, bring to a boil, then lower the heat to a simmer. Cut **8 ounces (250g) pollack fillet** into 4 pieces, add to the pan, and cook briefly until the fish is opaque. Add the mussels and **a handful of chopped cilantro**.

Enough for 2 generous bowls. Sweet, earthy, spicy.

A couple of variations on the chowder

A leek and clam chowder (an hour of your time but worth it)

Thinly slice 3 leeks, fry in butter till softened, then add 5 ounces (150g) bacon, chopped, making sure the leeks do not color. Cook 2 pounds (1kg) small clams with a glass of dry vermouth or wine in a large pot with a tight-fitting lid for a few minutes, till the clams open. Pull the clams out of their shells; it doesn't take long when you get into the swing of it. Add 1⅔ cups (400ml) of the clam cooking liquid to the leeks and bacon with ¾ cup (200ml) heavy cream, some black pepper, and a little chopped parsley. Remove half of the mixture and puree in a blender or food processor, then stir it back into the soup. Add the clams and serve with roughly torn crusty bread. For 4.

Corn and haddock. A cheat's chowder

Fry 2 chopped green onions in a little butter in a deep pan. Add a 14-ounce (400g) can of corn, 1 cup (250ml) heavy cream, and a handful of chopped parsley. Slide in a couple of pieces of skinned and boned smoked haddock (about 14 ounces / 400g total weight). Simmer for about 8 minutes, until the fish will flake easily. For 2.

Spiced Haddock Chowder

haddock, milk, onion, carrot, rutabaga,
potato, mustard seeds, turmeric, bay, parsley,
all-purpose flour, black peppercorns

Cut **2 haddock fillets** in half and place them in a deep pan with **2 cups
(500ml) milk, 2 bay leaves**, and **6 black peppercorns**. Bring the milk to
a boil and leave to infuse with the heat off and a lid on.

Coarsely chop **an onion** and fry it over low heat in **a little butter**.
Finely dice **a carrot, a medium-size rutabaga**, and **a waxy, yellow-
fleshed potato** and add to the onion. Fry for 5 to 10 minutes, till lightly
browned. Stir in **a teaspoon of mustard seeds** and **a teaspoon of
turmeric** and cook for 5 minutes.

Remove the haddock from the milk, reserving the milk. Scatter
2 tablespoons of all-purpose flour over the vegetables and cook for
a couple of minutes. Pour the infused milk into the pan and cook,
stirring continuously, until you have a thick sauce. Place the haddock
briefly in the pan to warm through, then add **a small handful of
chopped parsley** before serving.

For 2. Satisfying. A cold-weather dish.

A few thoughts on the miso soup

- Allowing the miso to boil will make it cloudy and alter its flavor, but a brief simmer will do no harm.
- Cook the pieces of meat for seconds rather than minutes, to keep them supple and rare.
- Shredded Savoy cabbage, broccoli rabe, and any of the Chinese greens would be perfect here instead of the kale.
- Add wide or thin ribbon noodles as you wish, or even cooked rice, to make a more substantial bowl of soup.

Miso Soup with Beef and Kale

white miso, sirloin steak, cavolo nero or
other kale, green onions, bouillon powder

Pull the leaves from the stalks of **3½ ounces (100g) cavolo nero or
other kale**. Shred them, then chop the stalks finely. Pour **a little oil**
into a shallow pan, add the chopped stems, and cook briefly, then add
an **8-ounce (240g) piece of sirloin steak**. Fry briefly and when it
browns, turn over and add **3 chopped green onions**. Brown the steak
on the other side, then remove from the pan and cover it, then pour
3⅓ cups (800ml) boiling water into the pan and stir. Add **a tablespoon
of bouillon powder** and **2 tablespoons of white (shiro) miso**, then the
cavolo nero leaves. Simmer until the greens wilt. Ladle into bowls,
slice the steak into thin strips, and drop into the broth.

For 2. Light and sustaining.

Roasted Beets and Tomato Spelt

beets, tomatoes, pearled spelt, garlic,
cilantro or parsley

Drizzle **4 small beets** with **a little oil**, wrap them in foil, and place in a roasting pan. Bake at 400°F (200°C) for 20 minutes. Open the foil, add **5 garlic cloves**, left whole, and **4 largeish tomatoes** and cook for another 30 minutes, until the beets and garlic are tender. Peel the garlic, then peel and halve the beets.

Boil **a rounded 1 cup (200g) pearled spelt** in 1⅔ cups (400ml) salted water for 20 minutes, then drain. Melt **a large knob of butter** in a frying pan, add the cooked spelt, and leave to toast lightly for a minute or two. Add the roasted beets, garlic, tomatoes, and some black pepper, stirring them in gently till the tomatoes burst. Stir in **a handful of torn cilantro or parsley.**

For 2. Frugal, sweet, and sharp, with the comfort of warm spelt.

Pea and Watercress
Soup, Shrimp Soldiers

peas, watercress, shrimp, baguette,
vegetable stock, shallots, soft butter, mace

Peel **2 medium shallots** and chop them quite finely, then let them cook
in **a little oil** over moderate heat till they are soft and translucent. Add
3½ cups (500g) shelled fresh peas then **4 cups (1 liter) vegetable stock.**
Stir and leave to simmer for 5 minutes.

Put most of the peas and the liquid into a food processor or blender
and puree till smooth. Add **a bunch of watercress** and continue
processing till smooth, then return to the rest of the soup. Making it
this way will give you a lightly textured soup, more interesting than
a totally smooth one. Check the seasoning.

For the shrimp soldiers, coarsely chop **5 ounces (150g) cooked
shrimp.** Cube 3½ tablespoons **(50g) butter** and mash the chopped
shrimp into it. Season with black pepper and **a pinch of ground mace.**

Thinly slice **a small baguette.** Spread the shrimp butter onto the
bread and bake for 10 minutes at 400°F (200°C), or cook under a
broiler if you prefer. Serve with the hot soup.

For 4. Sweet pea soup, crisp shrimp toasts.

In the frying pan

You melt a slice of butter in a wide, shallow pan. When bubbles appear around the edge, you slip in a fillet of fish and slowly let it cook, spooning the warm butter over and over. You watch the flesh change from pearl white to snow white and see the edges turn pale gold. You toss a salad or steam some green beans. You open a bottle of wine. You lift the fish onto a warm plate, add a little lemon juice and some chopped parsley to the butter in the pan, and let it foam before pouring it over the fish. Dinner is served.

A frying pan was the first piece of kitchen equipment I owned. A basic, shallow pan that saw many a meal, from a simple bacon sandwich to a full English breakfast. It helped me master everything from fish sticks to fried sea bass. I made risotto and fish cakes in it. Pork chops and hamburgers. Fried chicken and potatoes. I made curry in it, for heaven's sake. If we have only one pan, then it should probably be a frying pan.

Cooking in a shallow, long-handled pan is spirited, high-temperature cooking. A quick fix. We need to learn to control the heat. But first we must know our pan. A thin, cheap pan isn't ideal—the food burns too easily— but sometimes that is what we have. So we should get to know how the pan works, its hot spots and burning points, where food sticks on it and how long it takes to heat up. This isn't just "chuck it in and hope for the best" cooking. This is quick-fire food, but it needs the right pan, the right heat, and the right ingredients.

I have two frying pans now, one cast iron and so heavy I need both hands to lift it, the other nonstick and light as a feather. The cast-iron one is so well used it has developed its own nonstick patina and is what I use to fry potatoes, pieces of chicken, meatballs, burgers, and slices of bacon. It is great for homemade burgers that need slow cooking. The lighter pan is for fish, rösti, frittata, and flash-fried lamb's liver. Its slippery surface makes it ideal for an omelette.

If you make them regularly, it might be worth investing in a small omelette pan. Steel is the way to go. Never wash it—just a quick wipe with a paper towel. A new pan will stick initially. I get around this by heating a film of oil in it and letting it cool several times, then wiping it with a paper towel. This provides a seal that will stop your omelettes and frittata from sticking to the surface.

A good, flat pan with a heavy base, whether stainless steel or cast iron, is a food friend to have in the kitchen. For the full English breakfast, of course, with its bacon and sausage, black pudding, tomatoes, and egg, but for so much more. The pork steak or chop that needs to be watched as it cooks; the steak you don't want to grill; the leftover steamed rice you are resuscitating as fried rice, and for vegetables, chicken, and anything else that will cook in a few minutes. It's the lifesaver pan. The one we all start with. The one mum packs in our backpack when we leave home. Hopefully with a copy of this book.

A few favorites

Sole, asparagus, dill
Melt a thick slice of butter in a nonstick pan and add
a little olive oil. Add 6 asparagus spears, each spear cut
in half then into 3 or 4 pieces, and let them cook for a
minute or two. Scatter in a few roughly torn dill fronds,
then carefully lay 2 sole fillets, skin side down and side by
side, into the pan and spoon the asparagus and butter over
them. Season, then continue cooking for 4 or 5 minutes,
regularly spooning the hot butter and asparagus over the
fish, until the flesh becomes opaque.

Salmon, spinach, garlic
Fry a piece of salmon in a little oil in a shallow pan,
seasoning it with salt as you go. Remove the salmon to
a warm place (such as a warm plate with a cover). Put a
clove of garlic, peeled and very finely sliced, in the fish
pan, let it color lightly, then add a couple of handfuls of
spinach, toss them around in the hot pan, and add a slice
of butter and a squeeze of lemon. Serve under the fish.

A sweet, mildly spiced side dish for pretty much anything
Coarsely grate about 14 ounces (400g) carrots. Add a
crushed clove of garlic, a grated thumb-size lump of
fresh ginger, and a finely chopped hot chile. Melt a little
butter in a shallow pan, then add the carrots, toss gently
as they cook, then add a handful of chopped roasted

cashews, 4 tablespoons of heavy cream and the same of yogurt, then scatter with chopped cilantro leaves.

The sweetness of carrots, the coolness of mint
Gently scrub 1 pound (450g) spring carrots, removing their leaves as you go, then cook them in a little oil in a shallow pan. Keep the heat low, rolling them over now and again and letting them brown very slightly in patches. Add 2 tablespoons of chopped mint and 3 heaping tablespoons of yogurt to the pan. A side dish really, but satisfying enough with bread and cheese or cold cuts.

Potato and mushroom rösti
Grate some potatoes coarsely, then toss them with some beaten egg and flour. Season them with chopped thyme, shape into patties, and fry in hot butter till lightly crisp and golden. Drain on paper towels for a few minutes, then top with fried sliced mushrooms and crème fraîche.

Rösti and meat juices
Potato rösti are wonderful slipped under grilled lamb steaks or a piece of fillet steak. Something sensational about the crisp tangled straws of potato when they pick up some of the meat juices.

A mustard and tarragon sauce for steak

Put a tablespoon of Dijon mustard, the juice of a lemon, and about 20 tarragon leaves in a blender or food processor with 3½ tablespoons (50ml) olive oil and process to a thick purée. While the cooked steak rests, pour the juices from the pan into the tarragon sauce, blend, and serve with the steak.

A red chile and tomato sauce for steak

While your cooked steak rests, add a seeded and very finely chopped red chile to the pan, soften over moderate heat, then add a few chopped tomatoes and some salt and let the tomatoes cook down to a spicy red slush. Crush with a fork, stir in a handful of chopped cilantro, and serve with the steak.

Rice Cakes

leftover chilled risotto, egg, dried bread crumbs,
Emmentaler or Gruyère, lemon

Beat **an egg** lightly in a shallow dish. Spread **a couple of handfuls of dried bread crumbs** onto a plate. Cut the **Emmentaler or Gruyère** into small dice and fold into your **cold risotto.** Take generously mounded serving spoons of the mixture and roll into balls or flat patties (the shape is up to you), then drop them into the beaten egg followed by the bread crumbs.

Heat **a shallow layer of oil** in a frying pan and fry the cakes a few at a time till they are crisp on all sides, turning carefully (they are fragile) as you go. Serve 2 croquettes per person with **lemon halves.**

Crunch and soft. Melting cheese.

Note: It is essential to chill the rice quickly for this. Once the risotto is made, cool it quickly, if necessary by putting the pan into a sink of cold water. Chill thoroughly in the fridge overnight.

Another idea for vegetables with sausage

Brussels sprouts, sausage, and potato

Cut 7 ounces (200g) new potatoes into small coins, about four per potato, then let them cook in a little oil in a large frying pan. When they start to color, add 8 ounces (250g) good herby sausage meat in fat lumps, then cut 8 ounces (250g) Brussels sprouts into four and add to the pan. Continue frying till everything is toasted and the sprouts are soft but bright.

Beets with Sausage and Rosemary

beets, sausages, carrots, garlic, rosemary, red wine vinegar

Peel **1½ pounds (650g) raw beets**, cut into thick segments, then cut each segment in half. Do the same with **5 ounces (150g) carrots**, but don't peel them. Peel and slice **2 cloves of garlic**. Coarsely chop the needles from **3 sprigs of rosemary**. Fry the sliced vegetables, garlic, and rosemary in **3 tablespoons of peanut oil** over moderate heat till approaching tenderness (the vegetables need to retain a little crispness).

Cut **14 ounces (400g) good, herby fresh sausages** into three, then add them to the pan, letting them brown nicely. When the beets and carrots are tender, pour in **2 tablespoons of sweetish red wine vinegar**, check the seasoning, adding salt and pepper as you wish.

For 2 to 3. Sweet and sour, a sausage supper for an autumn night.

A few thoughts on the artichokes

- This is not a recipe where anything should be allowed to brown in the pan. Keep the colors pale and the flavors mild. Rinse the artichokes well of their preserving liquid.
- Tarragon is good here, as it always is with beans, and so would be mint. Add mint at the last minute, so it doesn't discolor much. You could cook your own artichokes if you wish. Prepare and boil them till tender, then add them, halved, to the melted butter and lemon as above.
- Swap the beans for Puy lentils and add more parsley for an earthier style.

For a change

Deep-fried artichokes, garlic mayo

Mix ¾ cup (100g) all-purpose flour with 2 tablespoons of sunflower oil, ¾ cup (175ml) sparkling mineral water, and a stiffly beaten egg white to make a tempura batter. Lightly flour then batter halved, bottled or canned marinated artichokes (they're also available loose from delicatessen counters). Lower them into hot, deep oil and fry till light and crisp. Drain on paper towels and serve with garlic mayonnaise and half a lemon.

Artichokes and Cannellini

artichokes, cannellini beans, green onions,
butter, lemon, parsley

Melt **3 tablespoons (40g) butter** in a shallow pan. As it melts, squeeze
in the **juice of half a lemon.** Chop **2 green onions** and let them
soften in the butter over moderate heat. Drain **a 10-ounce (300g) jar
of water-packed artichoke hearts,** then slice each one in half and add
to the butter.

Drain **a 14-ounce (400g) can of cannellini beans** and add to the pan.
Leave to quietly bubble over moderate heat till a sort of impromptu
creamy juice has developed. Season with salt, black pepper, and
perhaps **a little more lemon and parsley.**

For 2. A 10-minute dish with a gentle quality.

Basil Shrimp

shrimp, basil, pine nuts, lemon, olive oil

Make the basil dressing: put ¾ cup (20g) **basil leaves** into a food processor and process them to a rich, creamy sauce with ⅓ **cup (50g) pine nuts, the juice of a lemon**, and ½ **cup (120ml) olive oil**.

Cook **12 large, raw, shell-on shrimp** on a stove-top grill pan or a grill, or in a dry frying pan. Salt them generously as they cook and turn them regularly till their shells are pink. Remove the shrimp from the heat, toss them in the dressing, and eat immediately.

For 2. No forks, no knives. Shrimp with tasty shells to suck at and flesh to pick.

A few variations on the sausage mash

Classic sausage, cloud-like mash, sweet onion gravy

The classic. Make a quick onion gravy by cooking sliced onions in butter for 15 minutes, until softened, stirring from time to time, then add a little flour, let it color, and stir in a glass of dry Marsala and enough stock to make a rich, not-too-thick sauce.

Blood sausage, a cloud of potatoes, and apples

Boil or steam quite waxy potatoes. Peel, core, and slice an equal weight of slightly tart apples, preferably not as tart as Bramleys, then cook them in a little butter in a shallow pan. When they are soft, fluff them up with a fork. Drain the potatoes and beat them to a fluff with a little butter, then fold in the apple puree. Salt, not sugar. If using soft morcilla, best to bake. A drier, traditional blood sausage is better cooked in a shallow pan.

Toulouse sausage, butter bean mash

Broil or fry the sausages. Drain canned butter beans, heat them in a little fresh water, drain, then mash to a soft puree with butter and black pepper.

Chorizo and Sweet Potato Mash

chorizo sausages, sweet potatoes

Pierce **4 fresh chorizo sausages** all over with a fork, then brown in
a little oil in a shallow pan. Peel about **1 pound (500g) sweet potatoes**,
cut them into chunks about the size of ice cubes, and add to the pan.
Leave the sausages and potatoes to cook for 10 minutes, browning
nicely, then add ¾ **cup (200ml) water**, cover with a lid, and simmer for
10 minutes.

Remove the lid, turn up the heat, and allow half the liquid to evaporate,
then remove the sausages to a warm place. Mash the sweet potatoes with
a fork, adding **a thick slice of butter** as you go. Season the mash
with black pepper and salt, then serve with the sausages placed on top.

For 2. Smoke and silk.

A few thoughts on seafood balls

- Add enough bread crumbs to produce a mixture that will keep its shape when rolled into balls. You will need slightly different amounts depending on the type of bread you use. Do a trial ball first to make sure they hold together.
- Use a lowish heat, so the crab heats right through to the center.
- Be gentle when handling the cakes in the frying pan. Leave them to form a crisp crust on the base before carefully turning them over. That way, they should stay intact.

For a change

The shimmer of anchovy, the zest of lime

Rinse and finely chop 3 anchovies. Stir them into the crabmeat mixture opposite with the grated zest of a lime.

The warmth of smoke. A fish cake for winter

Use smoked fish such as mackerel instead of crab. Ditch the chile, and use a beaten egg to hold things together. Dill is better than cilantro for this.

Thai style

A little Thai green curry paste, stirred into the crab mixture opposite, produces a dazzling little crab cake.

The ease of canned fish

Sardines and salmon make an instant fish cake but are best when held together with mashed potato rather than bread crumbs. Use an equal volume of mashed potato and canned fish, then throw in chopped parsley, dill, and a little smoked paprika. Drain the fish well before adding it to the potato.

Crab Balls

crabmeat, chile, garlic, white bread,
cilantro, mirin

Put **a hot red chile**, including the seeds, into a food processor with
a garlic clove, 3½ ounces (100g) soft white bread, and **a large bunch
of cilantro** (about ⅔ ounce / 20g, including both the leaves and the
thinner stalks). Process till finely chopped, then transfer to a mixing
bowl and add **2 tablespoons of mirin** and **14 ounces (400g) lump
crabmeat**. Season with salt and black pepper. Mix well, then shape the
mixture into 12 small balls.

Warm **a very fine layer of sunflower or peanut oil** in a nonstick
frying pan, add the crab balls, and cook over low heat till they are
deep golden on the underside. Turn and continue cooking till they
are colored all over. Serve immediately with **halves of lime**.

For 3 to 4. Crisp, fragrant dumplings.

A few thoughts on the zucchini and gremolata

- Keep an eye on the bread crumbs, as they can burn in seconds. Different breads will soak up more or less butter, so keep some extra butter handy to add as necessary.
- As soon as the crumbs turn golden, transfer them to a dish.
- Don't try to fry the zucchini in the pan without wiping it clean and adding fresh oil or butter, as any remaining crumbs will burn.

Some variations

Introduce some basil in with the zucchini or the crumbs. I went for a passing breeze of garlic, but add more if you like.

Mushroom and zucchini, green and earthy

Replace the bacon with small mushrooms that you have sliced thinly, then tossed till dark and sticky in a little olive oil over moderate heat.

Tomato gremolata

Make the bacon gremolata as opposite. Slice medium-size tomatoes in half, cook for a few minutes in a little olive oil, then scatter the bacon mixture over them. Basil leaves in with the bread crumb mixture would be a fragrant addition here.

Zucchini with Bacon Gremolata

zucchini, bacon, rosemary, fresh bread crumbs, parsley, lemon, garlic

Cut **6 slices of bacon** into thick pieces, then fry them in a shallow pan, with **a little butter** if necessary, till they crisp lightly, then finely chop the needles from **a sprig of rosemary** and add them to the pan along with **a clove of crushed garlic**. Stir for a minute or two, then add **a couple of good handfuls of soft, fresh bread crumbs**. Add **more butter** if the crumbs prove thirsty. Let these cook till golden, turning them regularly, then toss in some **chopped parsley** if you have it, and the **finely grated zest of a small lemon**. Season generously.

When everything is crisp and golden, remove from the pan and wipe the pan with paper towels. Slice **4 medium to large zucchini** lengthwise, then cook them in **a little oil and butter**. When they are soft and translucent, scatter over the crumbs, heat gently, and serve. For 2.

A few ideas for poultry with beans

Chicken, chickpeas, parsnips. A winter dinner

Not exactly quick, but easy enough. Season 1½ pounds (750g) chicken pieces and brown them lightly in a little olive oil, then lift them out and set aside. Peel and chop 2 onions and let them soften in the chicken fat left in the pan. Add 6 slices of bacon, cut into short pieces, and continue cooking till the bacon is pale gold and the onions are soft and sweet. Peel and roughly cube a parsnip, add to the pan with some salt and pepper, then return the chicken to the pan. Add 2 14-ounce (400g) drained cans of chickpeas, pour in 4 cups (1 liter) of stock, and bring to a boil. Cover with a lid, transfer to an oven set at 350°F (180°C), and bake for 50 minutes.

Spiced roast chicken, creamy mashed beans

Crush a clove of garlic and put it in a mixing bowl with a teaspoon of red pepper flakes and 4 tablespoons of olive oil. Toss 4 chicken thighs in the seasoned oil and leave for half an hour. Roast the chicken thighs, seasoned with a little salt, at 400°F (200°C) for about 30 minutes.

Meanwhile, drain two 14-ounce (400g) cans of cannellini beans, add them to a saucepan, add ¾ cup (200ml) crème fraîche, and heat gently. Season with black pepper and salt, then crush with a potato masher to give a rich, creamy mash. Eat with the chile roast chicken.

Duck with Beans

duck breasts, cannellini beans,
rosemary, dry Marsala

Score the skin of **a couple of duck breasts**, then place them skin
side down in a hot nonstick pan and fry until golden brown. Drain
a 14-ounce (400g) can of cannellini beans and add them to the pan,
turning the duck over as you go. Tuck **a sprig of rosemary** into the
beans and pour in **5 tablespoons of dry Marsala**. Cover the pan and
leave to simmer for 5 minutes, till the skin is crisp and the flesh is still
pink within. Crush the beans lightly with a fork, season, and serve.

   For 2. Sweet pink meat, white beans.

A thought on frittatas

A frittata is cooked a little more slowly than an omelette or scrambled eggs. The filling is usually added as soon as the eggs go into the pan. I give the base a minute or two to set, then put the filling on before the center has time to set.

And a couple of ideas

Asparagus and tarragon

Lightly beat the eggs with a little chopped fresh tarragon. Trim and lightly cook a bunch of asparagus spears—the thinnest you can find—then add to the pan shortly after pouring in the egg.

Eggplant and thyme

Thinly slice a small to medium eggplant into disks. Soak them with olive oil, then scatter with thyme and salt. Cook under a broiler or in a stove-top grill pan, or, if you prefer, fry them in a nonstick pan. They should be really soft and tender. Add to the pan immediately after pouring in the egg.

Goat Cheese Frittata

goat cheese, eggs, spinach, butter, thyme, basil, rosemary

Beat **4 eggs** in a bowl and season generously. Add **a tablespoon of thyme leaves** and **a few roughly torn basil leaves**.

Heat the broiler. Melt **3½ tablespoons (50g) butter** in a small nonstick pan, about 8 inches (20cm) in diameter. Add **5 ounces (150g) spinach** and cook for about 1 minute, until the leaves soften. Add the spinach to the bowl with the eggs. Wipe the pan, then place **a thin slice of butter** in it. When it starts to sizzle add the egg mixture, then **5 ounces (150g) goat cheese**, sliced, and **a teaspoon of chopped rosemary leaves** and cook over low to moderate heat.

Once the omelette is partly set—this will take about 6 minutes— finish cooking it under the broiler until golden on top.

For 1. A tender, melting omelette.

A few variations on the ham and mustard

Ham sandwich, sour cream, and mustard mayo

Mix together equal quantities of mayonnaise and sour cream (the cream will sharpen and lighten it), then season with smooth Dijon mustard. Add to a classic ham sandwich with some torn iceberg lettuce and paper-thin, toothsome Cheddar. Crisp, soft, and familiar.

Ham, crème fraîche, two mustards

Fry a couple of ham steaks in butter, then remove them to warm plates. Add a small tub of crème fraîche to the pan, together with a couple of tablespoons of mustard—I suggest one each of Dijon and whole grain. Season with black pepper and a very little salt. Bring to a slow bubble, add a squeeze of lemon juice, and serve with the ham steaks.

Ham Steaks, Fava Beans, and Mustard Seeds

ham steaks, fava beans, butter, brown
mustard seeds

Boil ²/₃ cup (100g) shelled fava beans in deep, lightly salted water for
8 to 10 minutes, till tender, then drain them and return to the pan.
Using a fork or potato masher, crush the beans a little.

Melt 5 tablespoons (75g) butter in a shallow nonstick pan, let it sizzle,
then add two 4-ounce (125g) ham steaks. Cook for 3 or 4 minutes on
each side, spooning over the butter as you go. Remove the meat to
a warm plate, then add a teaspoon of brown mustard seeds to the
butter and let them cook briefly—they may start to pop. Stir in the
crushed fava beans and a grinding of black pepper. When all is sizzling,
briefly return the ham to the pan, then serve with the fava beans.

For 2. Pink meat, green beans.

A few ideas for the lamb and yogurt

- I usually grill marinated meats, but this spiced lamb is one you can cook on the stovetop. We cooked this with lamb marinated for an hour and also overnight. The difference was negligible.
- Some rice on the side would be good here, perhaps with lemon juice and cilantro leaves stirred through at the last moment.
- You could do this recipe with chicken breasts.
- Introduce a little ground cardamom. Finish with fresh cilantro leaves or mint.

Harissa

Mix a little harissa paste with enough olive oil to make a thick dressing, then stir in a teaspoon of brown sugar. Spread over the lamb and marinate for half an hour, or longer if you have time.

Red wine vinegar, garlic, crushed rosemary

Crush a clove of garlic, mix it with a little salt, some finely chopped rosemary, black pepper, and a touch of red wine vinegar. Rub this over the lamb, then grill.

Lamb with Yogurt and Turmeric

lamb steaks, garlic, fennel seeds, turmeric, ground coriander, yogurt

Set aside **4 lamb steaks, about 7 ounces (200g) each**. Peel and crush **a large clove of garlic** and pound it with a pestle and mortar with **half a teaspoon of fennel seeds**, then add **a teaspoon of turmeric** and **a teaspoon of ground coriander** and a little black pepper. Put **1 cup (250ml) yogurt** into a mixing bowl, then add the spice paste and mix well. Put the lamb steaks into the yogurt and leave for an hour or so.

Remove the steaks from the yogurt and fry in **peanut oil** in a hot, shallow pan, still with some of the spiced yogurt sticking to them, till a crust has developed, then turn and cook the other side. Serve with rice.

For 4. Earthy. Aromatic. Fragrant.

A few thoughts on the monkfish

- At the time of writing, monkfish isn't particularly sustainable, but any other firm white fish is suitable. Keep the pieces large and cook them only briefly.
- If the pan seems dry, add a trickle of olive oil before adding the fish.
- Once the clams go in, put the lid on the pan to encourage them to steam quickly. They are cooked as soon as they open. Discard any that don't open.

For a change

Brick-red chorizo, sweet mussels, a little vermouth

For a change, fry some chopped fresh chorizo in a deep pan, add the fish, as in the recipe opposite, and replace the clams with mussels in their shells, plus a little vermouth or dry sherry and just a little cilantro leaf. Cook, covered, until the mussels open.

Adding a rouille

Make a quick, cheaty rouille by stirring paprika and a little garlic puree into a good brand of mayonnaise. Add it to the dish as you serve it.

Monkfish with Pancetta and Clams

monkfish, pancetta, clams, smoked paprika, white vermouth

Cut **3½ ounces (100g) smoked pancetta** into large dice, then cook in a shallow pan over moderate heat. As the fat starts to run and the pancetta colors a little, toss **four 7-ounce (200g) pieces of monkfish tail** in **2 teaspoons of smoked paprika** mixed with a little salt and pepper. Add the pieces of fish to the pan and cook for 7 to 8 minutes, turning them as necessary. They need a little color on each side. Wash **7 ounces (200g) small clams**. Pour **1 cup (250ml) white vermouth** into the pan, let it bubble up, then add the clams. Cover the pan with a lid and cook briefly until the shells start to open. Discard any that remain shut. Check the seasoning and serve.

For 4. Pan juices that dazzle.

The richness of liver, the sweet-sourness of apple chutney

Warm a thin slice of butter and a glug of oil in a shallow pan. Lay 4 slices of lamb's liver in the sizzling pan and fry for a couple of minutes on each side (toasty brown edges are good, but the inside should still be rose pink). Remove to a warm plate and pour a small glass of dry Marsala or red wine into the pan. Bubble, stir, and scrape, then reduce by half over high heat. Stir in 4 tablespoons of coarse apple and onion chutney. Slide in the liver and serve.

Lamb's Liver, Onions, and Pecorino

lamb's liver, shallots, radishes,
red wine vinegar, parsley, butter, pecorino

Peel, halve, and very finely slice **10 ounces (300g) large shallots**. Melt **3 tablespoons (40g) butter** in a large nonstick frying pan. Add the shallots and fry, stirring regularly, for about 10 minutes, till soft and pale golden. Push to one side of the pan.

Cut **10 ounces (300g) lamb's liver** into small pieces and season generously. Add **a thin slice of butter** to the pan, then add the liver and fry for a maximum of 2 minutes on each side. Add **5 thinly sliced radishes**. Pour in **2 tablespoons of red wine vinegar** and add **a handful of parsley leaves**. Then add **½ cup (50g) finely grated pecorino**. Serve with skin-on mashed potato.

For 2. Good for you.

Eggplant Paneer

eggplant, paneer cheese, cherry tomatoes,
garam masala, yellow mustard seeds,
cilantro

Warm **2 tablespoons of sunflower or peanut oil** in a shallow pan or
wok. Cut **a large eggplant** into small dice (about ⅜ inch / 1cm), add
to the oil, and fry until golden and soft. As the eggplant colors, halve
7 ounces (200g) cherry tomatoes and add them to the pan. As they
soften, tear or chop **8 ounces (250g) paneer cheese** and add that to
the pan, too. Scatter over **a tablespoon of garam masala, a tablespoon
of yellow mustard seeds**, and a little salt. Continue frying for a
couple of minutes, till the paneer is very lightly colored, then stir in
a handful of cilantro leaves. Serve with steamed rice.

For 4. Cheerful, singing flavors.

Parsnip Rösti

parsnips, potato, shallots, balsamic vinegar,
egg, cream cheese, all-purpose flour, sugar,
green peppercorns

Peel **8 large shallots**, slice them in half, and unfurl the layers. Warm
a thin slice of butter and **4 tablespoons of olive oil** in a shallow pan,
add the shallots, and fry over low to moderate heat till soft and pale
gold. Stir in **3 tablespoons of balsamic vinegar** and **a tablespoon of
sugar**. Cook over low heat until the shallots are sweet and sticky, then
set aside but keep warm.

Coarsely grate **8 ounces (250g) parsnips** and **a medium potato** into
a bowl. Lightly beat **an egg** and add it to the bowl with **2 tablespoons
of all-purpose flour**. Mix well and press the grated vegetables into
6 small, thin patties. Heat **a thin film of peanut oil or butter** in a
frying pan, add the patties, and fry till crisp and golden. Remove,
drain briefly on paper towels, and divide among plates.

Season **8 ounces (250g) cream cheese** with **a few bottled green
peppercorns**, a little black pepper, and some salt. Place a heaping
spoonful of the cream cheese on top of each pancake and add some
of the warm shallots. Serve immediately. For 3 to 4.

A few thoughts on the potatoes

This is a dish born from an empty cupboard, and to add too many ingredients would miss the point. A chopped chile at the start would add interest, as would a handful of torn basil at the end. Other appropriate additions include chopped or sliced garlic, added with the onion, a pinch of ground paprika, some fennel seeds, or a little smoked garlic. An egg or two, cracked on top at the end, will bring all the ingredients together.

Poor Man's Potatoes

potatoes, peppers, onion, vegetable stock

Wipe **1 pound (500g) new potatoes** and halve them. Heat **a little olive oil** in a shallow pan, place the potatoes in it cut side down, and leave them to cook. Halve and seed **2 large yellow or red peppers**, cut them into long strips, and add to the pan. Peel and finely slice **a large yellow or red onion** and add it to the potatoes and peppers together with **a large knob of butter**. Leave to cook, with the occasional stir, until the potatoes are nicely golden and the onion is starting to soften. Pour in **1²/₃ cups (400ml) vegetable stock**, bring to a boil, season, then cover with a lid and let it simmer enthusiastically for 20 minutes. Once the stock has almost disappeared, crush a few of the potatoes with a fork, allowing them to absorb the last drops of liquid.

For 2. Frugal, rich, nourishing.

A few variations on the steak with pasta

Lamb and leeks

Sauté a couple of finely sliced, medium-size leeks in butter till they are soft but not colored. This is often done with a layer of parchment paper over the leeks and a lid, so they sweat as much as fry. Broil or panfry a lamb steak, slice into thinnish strips, then toss with the cooked leeks and a little grated Caerphilly cheese. Serve over fettuccine or tagliatelle.

Grilled duck and red onions

Peel and slice a couple of red onions, then let them cook in a little butter and oil till soft. Broil or panfry a duck breast till tender, slice into thin strips, then toss with the onions, a tablespoon of red wine vinegar, and a handful of chopped parsley. Serve with the pasta.

Philly Cheese Steak with Tagliatelle

skirt steak, tagliatelle, provolone
piccante cheese, onions, beef dripping

Peel and thinly slice **2 medium onions** and fry them to a soft, pale
gold in **2 tablespoons of oil** or **preferably beef dripping**. Cook
5 ounces (150g) tagliatelle in a deep pan of salted water, then drain.
Grate **6 ounces (180g) provolone piccante**. Slice **8 ounces (250g) skirt
steak** into finger-thin strips, then add to the onions, letting the strips
cook briefly, keeping their insides pink. Toss the steak, onions, and
pasta, then add the grated provolone piccante and a little black pepper.
    For 2 to 3. Intensely satisfying. Piquant and a good value.

A few thoughts on the pork with figs

- Make certain the chops brown nicely on both sides before you introduce the cider; that way, the pan juices will be tastier.
- Use figs that are lightly ripe so they don't collapse during cooking. If you have tiny ripe figs, you could leave them whole.
- Include a little chopped thyme or rosemary with the chops.
- Swirl a knob of butter into the juices at the end.

For a change

The sweetness of pork chops, the glow of translucent pears

Cook pork chops in a little butter and oil in a shallow pan. As the chops start to color, add sliced, unpeeled pears and continue cooking till tender and translucent. Remove the chops and fat, then add a small wineglass of both vegetable stock and cider, reduce by bubbling, then spoon over the chops. On the side? A salad of endive and walnuts.

Ripe plums, rosemary

Finely chop a tablespoon of rosemary leaves, then mash them with a thick slice of butter, a little salt, and some black pepper. Melt half of the butter in a shallow pan, then, once it starts to sizzle, add 2 large pork chops and let them color nicely on both sides. Keep the heat moderate to low while they cook right through. As the chops approach the end of their cooking time, add 4 halved and pitted plums and the rest of the rosemary butter. Once they are soft and the pork cooked, serve.

Pig and Fig

pork chops, cider, figs

Season **2 pork chops**. Melt **a little butter** in a shallow pan and, once it starts to sizzle, brown the chops on each side. The fat should color nicely. Pour in **1 cup (250ml) dry hard cider**, let it bubble, then lower the heat, halve **4 or so small figs**, add them to the pan, and cover with a lid. Continue cooking for about 5 minutes, then remove the lid and let the cider reduce by about half.

For 2. Sweet, succulent, fruity.

A few variations on the potatoes and egg

Pistachio, pumpkin, pumpkin seed

Fry pumpkin instead of potato, steaming it for a few minutes first, then add pumpkin seeds and shelled pistachios for a bit of crunch.

Roasted Jerusalem artichoke, walnut, and egg

Jerusalem artichokes can be peeled, steamed, diced, and browned in butter, then scattered with chopped walnuts and salt. Slide a fried egg onto the plate.

Potatoes with Hazelnuts and Egg

new potatoes, hazelnuts, egg yolks, butter, chives

Wash and coarsely chop **1 pound (500g) new potatoes**. Warm **5 tablespoons (75g) butter** with **a couple of glugs of peanut or olive oil** in a shallow pan over moderate heat, add the potatoes, and fry at a gentle sizzle till golden brown all over and tender. Coarsely chop **²/₃ cup (100g) hazelnuts**, add them to the potatoes, and let them color a little. Season lightly with salt and black pepper. Add **4 tablespoons of chopped chives** and transfer to a flameproof dish.

Separate **4 eggs**, dropping the yolks into the potatoes, then place under a hot broiler for 3 or 4 minutes, till the yolks are warm but not set.

For 2. The scrunch of hazelnuts.

A few thoughts on the pork ribs

- Choose the smallest pork ribs you can find—sometimes known as baby back ribs. They need to cook quickly.
- Watch carefully when browning the ribs, and when adding the marinade to the pan, as they can burn easily. Keep the heat moderate.
- Try the same marinade for larger ribs and bake them slowly in a low oven. Serve with rice or bread for mopping up any sauce.
- This recipe works with chicken drumsticks too. Just cook them a little longer.

Other ideas

A red fruit version

Use cranberry jelly in place of the pomegranate molasses. Add a little crushed juniper and a splash of cranberry juice and cook as opposite.

Aniseed and honey

A traditional rib recipe might include molasses, cayenne pepper, mustard powder, tomato ketchup, onion, garlic, smoked paprika, cider vinegar, and apple juice. The only way to find the perfect ratio for you is to keep tasting as you go along. My knee-jerk rib recipe is mostly honey, to which I add half the amount of oyster sauce, then plenty of crushed garlic, some red pepper flakes, a little ground star anise, salt, and black pepper. It works best as a long, slow bake, but also in the version opposite.

Quick Pork Ribs with Honey and Pomegranate Molasses

baby back pork ribs, honey, pomegranate molasses, dark soy sauce, red pepper flakes, mirin

Mix together **3 tablespoons of honey, 2 tablespoons of dark soy sauce, a teaspoon of red pepper flakes, a tablespoon of pomegranate molasses**, and **2 tablespoons of mirin**. Slice **10 ounces (300g) small pork ribs into individual ribs**, then toss them in the dressing.

Brown the ribs quickly in **a little oil** in a shallow pan over moderate heat, turning them regularly. As soon as they start to caramelize, pour over any remaining marinade and let it bubble briefly, taking care not to let it burn, then add ½ **cup (100ml) water**. Cover the pan with a lid and cook for about 5 minutes. Remove the lid and continue cooking for a couple of minutes, till the ribs are dark and glossy.

For 2. Sticky, spicy, finger-licking stuff.

Another idea for the frittata

Blood sausage frittata

Melt a thick slice of butter in a small nonstick frying pan. Remove the skin from 7 ounces (200g) blood sausage and crumble the sausage into the hot butter, leaving it to color to a deep golden brown. Lightly beat 3 eggs, add about 3 tablespoons of coarsely chopped parsley, then pour the mixture over the sausage. Add ½ cup (50g) finely grated Parmesan cheese. Cook over fairly low heat till the bottom has formed a golden crust. The center will hopefully still be wobbly. Slip the pan under a hot broiler till the frittata has set and the top is lightly colored. Cut into wedges to serve.

Spiced Root Frittata

parsnips, beets, carrots, onion, cardamom, cumin, coriander, red pepper flakes, black mustard seeds, canned tomatoes, eggs, all-purpose flour

Peel and grate **a total of 8 ounces (250g) of mixed root vegetables, such as parsnips, beets,** and **carrots.** Peel, then finely shred **a small onion** and add to the grated roots. Stir in **2 tablespoons of all-purpose flour, half a teaspoon each of ground cardamom, cumin,** and **coriander, a pinch of red pepper flakes,** and **half a teaspoon of black mustard seeds.** Mix in **half a 14-ounce (400g) can of chopped tomatoes,** drained. Lightly beat **4 eggs** and add those too.

Warm **a thin pool of butter** in a 8-inch (20cm) shallow nonstick pan, then add the egg and tomato mixture. Cook till a golden crust has formed on the base but the top is still quite liquid in the center, then place under a preheated broiler and cook for 2 minutes or so, till lightly set.

For 2. A soft tangle of sweet vegetables held together by lightly spiced eggs.

Salmon with Artichokes

salmon, marinated artichokes, parsley,
dill, lemon

Grill, bake, or shallow-fry **12 ounces (350g) salmon**, then set aside.
Slice **4 marinated artichoke hearts** in half.

Flake the cooked salmon, then warm in **a little olive oil** in a shallow
nonstick pan. Add the artichokes, then season with **whole parsley
leaves, a little chopped dill**, and **a squeeze of lemon**.

For 2. Light, clean, delicate.

Two variations on the sardines and potatoes

Sweet potatoes, the crunch of nuts

The recipe opposite works very nicely with sweet potatoes cut into small cubes. Once the potatoes are soft inside and are starting to color, toss in a few cashew nuts, let them color lightly, then add chopped chives and the crumbled sardines.

Earthy Jerusalem artichokes, a spritz of lemon

Slice well-scrubbed Jerusalem artichokes in half and fry them in butter and a little oil till they are soft inside and crisply golden on the outside. Add a generous amount of chopped parsley, a can of drained and broken-up sardines, and a good squeeze of lemon juice.

Sardines, Potatoes, and Pine Nuts

canned sardines, new potatoes, pine nuts, green onions, parsley

Scrub **14 ounces (400g) new potatoes** and quarter them. Brown the potatoes in a heavy frying pan in **a little olive oil**. This will take a good 15 minutes at low to moderate heat with the occasional stir.

Chop **3 green onions** into rings and roughly crush **3½ tablespoons (30g) pine nuts**. When the cut sides of the potatoes are crusted and golden, add the green onions and cook briefly till soft. Add **a large handful of torn parsley**, the pine nuts, and a little black pepper. Lastly, drain **3½ ounces (100g) canned sardines in olive oil**, letting them crumble a little, and add to the pan.

For 2, as a light meal. Crunchy nuts, toasted potatoes.

A few thoughts on the sausage balls

- Get a good sausage. Perhaps something with plenty of parsley and pepper in it. To peel it, slit the casing from one end to the other with a knife, pull the casing apart, and squeeze the filling out into a bowl.
- Beef up the seasoning a bit if you like, with some chopped thyme, crushed garlic, black pepper, or grated Parmesan.
- Use a good-quality ready-made stock. Supermarkets and some butchers sell it in tubs.
- Add chopped dill to the meatballs and the sauce.
- Use crème fraîche instead of cream or, for a less rich dish, use just stock and forget the cream.
- For a milder version use chicken stock instead of beef.
- Serve with wide ribbon noodles such as pappardelle.
- Instead of using store-bought sausages, season plain sausage meat as you wish. Try juniper, thyme, garlic, cumin, or ground cardamom.

The freshness of lemon, the warmth of rosemary

Season the mixture opposite with very finely chopped rosemary, crushed garlic, and a little grated lemon. Shape into balls and fry in olive oil, adding a little butter and lemon juice to the pan juices at the end.

Sausage Balls, Mustard Cream Sauce

sausages, beef stock, heavy cream,
Dijon mustard, chives

Remove the casings from **1 pound (450g) really good-quality fresh sausages**. Roll the sausage meat into about 24 balls, slightly smaller than a golf ball. Warm **a little oil** in a nonstick frying pan over moderate heat and cook the balls till they color, turn them over, and continue cooking till they are evenly browned. Pour off any excess fat and pour in **2 cups (500ml) beef stock**. Bring to a boil, allow to reduce a little, then pour in **1 cup (250ml) heavy cream** and stir in **a tablespoon of Dijon mustard**. Season with salt and pepper and continue cooking for 15 to 20 minutes. Remove the balls to warm dishes, then turn the heat up under the sauce (there will be lots) and let it reduce a little. It will not thicken. Pour the sauce over the meatballs and serve with a fork and a spoon. **A few snipped chives** can be added if you wish.

For 2 to 3. My favorite meatballs, ever.

A few variations on the spelt cakes

Spelt with pork

Brown a pork chop, either from the loin or neck, in a little oil. Add a diced apple—it's quite good with the skin left on—and a couple of leaves of sage. Add the pearled spelt, then pour over vegetable or chicken stock and simmer for about 25 minutes, till the spelt has swelled and the chop is tender.

Spelt risotto

Use pearled spelt in place of rice in a risotto. Melt a thick slice of butter in a pan, add a finely chopped shallot and some pearled spelt, then stir in hot stock as if you were making risotto. Work on a rounded 1 cup (200g) of pearled spelt to 4 cups (1 liter) of hot stock. Mushrooms would be good here, chopped into plump nuggets and fried with the shallot before you add the spelt. Finish with grated goat cheese.

Spelt, Basil, and Ricotta Cakes

pearled spelt, ricotta, egg yolks, basil, tomatoes

Boil **1⅓ cups (250g) pearled spelt** in deep, lightly salted water for 20 minutes, drain, and set aside.

Stir in **1 cup (250g) ricotta, a couple of egg yolks, 1 cup (20g) whole basil leaves**, salt, and black pepper. Leave for 15 minutes, then shape into eight round patties. Fry gently in **a little olive oil** in a nonstick frying pan until golden and crisp on the outside. If they appear to be browning too quickly, then lower the heat a little and cover with a lid. Serve with **thick slices of ripe tomato** and **a drizzle of olive oil**.

Makes 8 small patties, enough for 2 to 4. Gentle and mild, but with big peppery bites of basil.

A few variations on the sesame lamb

A classic

Roll the lamb mixture opposite into balls. Seal them in a little oil in a shallow pan over moderate heat, then transfer to an ovenproof dish. Pour tomato sauce over them, then bake till the sauce is bubbling and the balls are cooked right through.

Mushrooms, cream. An autumnal version

Make half the quantity of lamb mixture opposite and mix it with the same amount of ricotta cheese. Shape into patties and fry in a little oil, then remove from the pan. Fry sliced cremini mushrooms in the pan until golden, adding more oil if you need to, then pour in a little brandy and scrape up the stickings from the bottom of the pan. Add crème fraîche or heavy cream. Stir, simmer for a minute or two, then pour the mixture over the patties and bake for a few minutes to cook the meat right through.

Mint and golden raisins. The crunch of pine nuts

Add fresh or even dried mint to the ground lamb mixture opposite, plus a few golden raisins and some pine nuts. Shape into patties and fry all the way through, then remove from the pan. Add a good thick slice of butter and some lemon juice to the pan, stir to scrape up the tasty pan-stickings, then pour the mixture over the patties and serve.

Spiced Sesame Lamb with Cucumber and Yogurt

ground lamb, black mustard seeds,
white sesame seeds, green onions,
garam masala, cucumber, yogurt, mint

Put **1 pound (500g) ground lamb** in a bowl, add **a tablespoon of black mustard seeds, 4 tablespoons of white sesame seeds**, salt, pepper, **2 green onions**, chopped, and **2 teaspoons of garam masala**. Mix well, then divide into 8 and flatten into large patties, each about ¼ inch (6mm) thick.

Heat **a little olive oil** in a shallow nonstick pan, place the patties in it, cooking approximately 2 at a time, and fry for a minute or two on each side, till patchily golden.

Take long, thin shavings from **a cucumber** with a vegetable peeler and season with a little salt and pepper. Stir **a tablespoon of chopped mint** into **4 tablespoons of yogurt**.

For each person, place 2 patties on a warm plate and top with a few curls of cucumber and a spoonful of yogurt.

For 4. Savory, aromatic lamb cakes, a trickle of yogurt.

A few thoughts on the eggs and squash

- Steaming or boiling the squash before frying ensures it is truly tender and fluffy.
- Keep the heat moderate when cooking the spices so they do not burn.
- Keep the eggs lightly cooked; the runny yolk forms a dressing for the squash.
- Serve with sausages instead of eggs. Try with parsnips or carrots instead of squash. Use the spiced squash as a side dish for grilled chicken, or stir it into a pilaf.

And a few variations

Buttered poached eggs and herbs

Melt 3½ tablespoons (50g) butter in a shallow pan. As it bubbles, slide in 4 lightly poached eggs. Scatter them with a couple of tablespoons of chopped herbs and a few drops of lemon juice and baste gently. Serve immediately.

English muffins, cheese, poached eggs

Toast and generously butter split English muffins. Top them with poached eggs, pile on grated cheese, then bake or grill till melted.

Eggs and ham

Same as above but place a piece of ham under the poached eggs and use sliced provolone cheese on top of them.

Spiced Eggs with Squash

squash, mustard seeds, garam masala, eggs

Peel **a medium-size squash, such as red kuri or butternut**, and remove and discard the seeds. Cut the flesh into small bite-size pieces. Steam the squash over boiling water till tender to the point of a knife, then drain and set aside.

Warm **4 tablespoons of olive, canola, or peanut oil** in a deep frying pan, then add **a tablespoon of mustard seeds**. Add the cooked squash and let it color. Stir gently, taking care not to break up the pieces, then sprinkle over **a tablespoon of garam masala**. Continue to cook for a few minutes, till fragrant, then remove to 2 warm plates. Break **2 eggs** into the pan and fry till just cooked. Slide them carefully on top of the squash.

For 2. Sweet, autumnal.

Steak with Miso

rib-eye or sirloin steak, white miso, shallot,
tarragon, chervil, cider vinegar, butter

Fry **2 rib-eye or sirloin steaks** in **a little butter and olive oil** in a shallow
pan, turning and basting regularly (I turn mine every 2 minutes and
baste almost continuously). When the meat is done to your liking, lift
from the pan and set aside to rest on a warm plate. Add **4 tablespoons
(60g) butter** to the pan, let it sizzle briefly, then stir in **a shallot**, finely
chopped, and let it soften for a minute, stirring occasionally and
scraping the browned steak juices from the pan. Add **2 tablespoons
of white (shiro) miso** and **a tablespoon of cider vinegar** and whisk.
(If it looks like the sauce is splitting, add **a spoonful of hot water** and
whisk.) Stir in **a tablespoon of chopped tarragon** and **a tablespoon of
chopped chervil.**
    For 2. Steak with deeply savory juices.

James's Potato Tortilla

egg, potato, shallot

Cut **an unpeeled medium to large potato** into very, very small dice—
a *brunoise*, as they say in cheffy circles. Melt **a thick slice of butter**
in a small, shallow 6-inch (15cm) pan. Add the potatoes and cook till
soft and pale gold, about 10 minutes. Add **a large shallot**, peeled and
very, very finely sliced, and cook for 3 to 5 minutes to soften. Beat **an
egg** with seasoning, then pour it over the onion and potato. Cook
for about 3 minutes, until it puffs up around the edges, then finish
cooking it under a hot broiler, leaving it liquid in the center.

For 1. A potato, a shallot, a little butter, and an egg.

Note: Of all the recipes James and I have worked on together, this is
the one that I think of as his and his alone. There is something quite
perfect about it. Maybe it's the Spanish in him. Whatever, this is one
of the loveliest things I have ever eaten.

Tomatoes, Charred Onions, and Steak

sirloin steak, butter, green onions, tomatoes

Melt **4 tablespoons (60g) butter** in a very large shallow pan and season a **1-pound (450g) piece of sirloin steak** with salt and black pepper. When the butter is sizzling, brown the meat on both sides, remove, and set aside. Cut **3 large green onions** in half lengthwise and add them to the pan, letting them brown a little.

Halve **1½ pounds (650g) large tomatoes**, then add them to the pan, covering with a lid and letting them cook for 10 to 15 minutes or so, till soft and lightly browned here and there. Season generously, pressing the tomatoes lightly with a spoon so their juices run into the pan.

Now that the steak has rested, slice the meat thickly, then tuck the pieces among the softening tomatoes. Continue cooking briefly, then serve.

For 2 to 3. Rare meat, ripe tomatoes, pan juices.

Some thoughts on the pork kebabs

- The mango should be ripe, but not so much so that it is too tender to cook. Otherwise it will fall off the skewers.
- If mango doesn't tempt, try plums. They go very well with pork.
- I have used pork shoulder with great success, but any cut will work, although the fatty cuts will produce a lot of smoke if broiled.

Other ideas for pork kebabs

Lip-tingling pork, cool pomegranate-flecked yogurt

Coarsely grate half a small cucumber, then put into a colander and season generously with salt. Leave for 20 minutes, then squeeze out the excess water. Fold the cucumber into ¾ cup (200ml) yogurt, then stir in a small handful of fresh mint leaves, the seeds from half a pomegranate, and a generous grinding of black pepper. Thread 7 ounces (200g) cubed pork steaks onto flat wooden skewers. Using a pestle and mortar, mash half a teaspoon of sea salt flakes, a quarter teaspoon of black peppercorns, and a large, peeled clove of garlic to a coarse-grained, wet powder, then rub all over the pork. Drizzle lightly with olive oil, then broil, browning nicely on all sides. Eat with the pomegranate yogurt.

Miso pork kebabs

Put a lightly heaping tablespoon of white (shiro) miso in a small saucepan over moderate heat. Stir in 3 tablespoons mirin until the miso dissolves. Toss the pork in the mixture, then thread onto skewers and grill till the edges are deep glossy brown.

Greengage and honey

Brush the cubed pork with a mixture of honey and Dijon mustard and season generously with salt. Thread onto wooden skewers, alternating pork with greengage plum. Cook as opposite.

Pork and Mango Kebabs

pork shoulder, whole-grain mustard,
mango, lemon

Cut **14 ounces (400g) pork shoulder** into large cubes, about 1¼ inches
(3cm) in diameter. Put them in a dish with **a tablespoon of oil** and
2 tablespoons of whole-grain mustard, add a grinding of black
pepper and plenty of salt, and mix thoroughly so that each piece of
meat is covered with a light coating of mustard.

Peel **a ripe mango.** Remove the flesh from the pit in the largest
pieces possible, then cut into large cubes, roughly the same size as
the meat. Thread the pieces of meat and mango onto wooden or
metal skewers, pushing the pieces close together.

Brush **a thin film of oil** over a heavy nonstick or cast-iron frying
pan and place over moderate heat. When the oil is hot, place the
skewers in the pan and let the meat color appetizingly, then turn and
cook the other side. Check that the meat is cooked right through,
then serve. (You may find a thin spatula useful to slide under the
meat and mango where it sticks slightly to the pan.) A fat squeeze of
lemon will make it sing.

For 2. The warmth of mustard. The lusciousness of mango.

On the side of the chicken wings

Rice, plainly steamed. No spice.

And a few variations

Chicken, light soy, smoky red pepper flakes, the warmth of maple syrup

Mix 2 tablespoons of maple syrup with 1 tablespoon of light soy sauce and another of lemon juice. Stir in 2 large pinches of crumbled red pepper flakes. Baste the grilling chicken pieces with this as they cook.

Crunchy wings, garlic mayo, fingers to lick

Dust the wings with seasoned flour and deep-fry or panfry till the outside is crisp. Drain briefly on paper towels, then serve with a pot of garlic mayonnaise.

Citrus and heat, one for chile heads

Puree a whole clementine, with its skin, in a food processor with as much habanero chile as you can take (they are very, very hot), a little mild mustard, then red wine vinegar and sugar to taste. If you add too much chile, chuck in another clementine. Pour into a saucepan, bring to a boil, then simmer till thick. Boil down and use as a marinade for chicken wings before grilling or roasting.

Chicken Wings, Katsu Sauce

chicken wings, onion, ginger, garlic, carrots, tomatoes, honey, soy sauce, garam masala, curry powder, chile, chicken stock

In a food processor, combine **a peeled onion, a cork-size piece of peeled fresh ginger, 3 cloves of garlic, 8 ounces (250g) carrots, 12 ounces (350g) tomatoes, 3 tablespoons runny honey**, and **3 tablespoons of soy sauce**. Mix in **2 tablespoons of garam masala** and **2 tablespoons of mild curry powder** and **a small, hot red chile**. Puree to a paste, then fry for 5 minutes. Add **12 chicken wings** and brown lightly, adding **a little peanut or sunflower oil** if necessary, then pour in **1⅔ cups (400ml) chicken stock** and simmer for 30 minutes.

Remove the wings to a nonstick frying pan and cook over moderate heat to crisp them. Serve with the sauce.

For 2. Crisp little wings. Hot sweet gravy.

A few variations on the potted shrimps

Smoked salmon, sour cream, dark rye

Mix together equal quantities of sour cream and mayonnaise, then season with salt, pepper, and a few capers. Peel a sweet red onion and slice it into very fine rings. Spread the sour cream mixture onto squares of sticky dark rye bread, add a little of the onion (taking care not to add too much), then cover generously with smoked salmon. Top with a second piece of rye bread or serve open.

Smoked trout, wasabi

Mash some smoked trout into a coarse paste with a fork. Add about half the amount of cream cheese, then mix in a good squeeze of wasabi paste, a shot of lemon juice, and a little salt. Keep tasting and adding more wasabi until it is hot enough for you. Spread thickly on sliced farmhouse bread and cover with a single layer of very finely sliced white daikon or radish. Then spread the smoked trout paste on top. I like to use a light, moist brown bread for this one.

Smoked mussels, gherkins

Finely slice a couple of large shallots and cook in butter in a shallow pan. When they are soft, sweet, and pale gold, add a couple of coarsely sliced large gherkins, then a can of smoked mussels, drained of their oil. Sandwich in 2 small, floury rolls.

Potted Shrimp, Cucumber, Dill, and Sourdough

potted shrimp, cucumber, dill,
lemon, sourdough bread

Add **5 ounces (150g) potted shrimp (small shrimp packed in butter)**
to a nonstick frying pan and let them cook briefly in their butter. Peel
half a cucumber, slice it very thinly with a vegetable peeler, then toss
with **a handful of torn or chopped dill**. Add **a good squeeze of lemon**.
 Toast **2 large slices of sourdough bread**, then top with the shrimp
and cucumber. For 2.

Herb Ricotta Cakes

ricotta, eggs, flour, butter, chives, chervil,
parsley, avocado, lemon, sprouts

Make a topping for the cakes. Halve, peel, pit and finely dice
an avocado, put it in a bowl, then add **the juice of a lemon**, a little
black pepper, and **a couple of glugs of olive oil**. Cover and set aside.

To make the ricotta cakes, separate **3 eggs**, putting the whites
into a bowl large enough to beat them in later and the yolks into
another bowl. Add **1 cup (250g) ricotta** to the egg yolks, then stir
in **6½ tablespoons (50g) all-purpose flour** and **2 tablespoons (30g)
melted butter**. Chop **a handful of chives, chervil**, and **parsley** and stir
them in, then season with a little salt.

Beat the egg whites till light and fluffy, then stir into the ricotta
mixture. Melt **a little butter** in a nonstick frying pan over moderate heat.
Take a sixth of the ricotta mixture and pat it lightly into a small cake
about 2½ inches (6cm) across, using the back of a spoon. Make 2 more.
When the butter sizzles lightly, add the cakes. When the cakes have
colored lightly on the bottom, flip them over with a thin spatula (do this
quickly and confidently and they won't break), then let the other side
become a soft, pale gold. The full cooking time shouldn't be more than
a few minutes. Repeat with the remaining mixture.

continued

Remove the cakes with a thin spatula, let rest briefly on paper towels, then transfer to a plate. Place **a heaping tablespoon of ricotta** on each cake, divide the avocado mixture among them, then add **a few sprouts** and serve.

Makes 6. Light, tender, fresh little pancakes.

A few thoughts on the spiced rice

Once the rice is soft and tender, add the lightly beaten egg. The trick is to leave it in place for a minute or so for the egg to partially set before stirring and breaking it up among the rice. It is easy to overcook, so once the egg has had its initial setting time, stir briefly and regularly to break it up and distribute it evenly among the rice.

And a few variations

Green spiced rice

Use green curry paste instead of the red. Before you add the carrot and rice to the pan, fry a few sliced button mushrooms in the butter, letting them color lightly. At the very end, fold in a little chopped cooked spinach, or perhaps some cooked peas. Fava beans will work if there are no edamame.

Fridge rice

Although I don't believe fried rice should be made with any old leftovers you might find lurking in the fridge, it is nevertheless a good way to use up leftover sausages, thinly sliced bacon, and finely chopped cooked greens. The trick is never to add more than one type of leftover at a time.

Quick Spiced Rice

basmati rice, Thai red curry paste, edamame, carrot, vegetable stock, eggs, cilantro

Cook **5 ounces (150g) podded edamame beans** in boiling water, then drain and set aside. Pour **1⅔ cups (400ml) vegetable stock** into a saucepan, add **2 tablespoons of Thai red curry paste**, then **1 cup (200g) basmati rice**. Bring to a boil, cover with a lid, and leave to simmer for 10 minutes, till almost tender and most of the liquid has been absorbed.

Melt **a slice of butter** in a frying pan, add the rice together with **a large carrot**, coarsely grated, and the reserved edamame. Stir regularly till the rice is moist but no longer wet, then add **3 eggs**, lightly beaten. Season. Continue cooking, leaving the rice in place for a few minutes to let the egg color, then stir it gently to break the mixture up. Carry on for a couple of minutes till the egg is lightly cooked and visible in patches throughout the rice. Toss in **a handful of cilantro**.

For 2 to 3. A little lifesaver.

Root Vegetable Patties
with Spiced Tomato Sauce

parsnips, carrots, onion, egg, cardamom, cumin,
coriander, red pepper flakes, black mustard
seeds, canned tomatoes, garlic

Mix together **a scant teaspoon of ground cardamom, half a teaspoon of ground cumin, and half a teaspoon of ground coriander**. Stir in **a large pinch of red pepper flakes, a teaspoon of black mustard seeds**, and **a tablespoon or so of peanut oil**. Toast half this spice mix in a pan for a couple of minutes. Crush **a garlic clove** and add to the pan with **a 14-ounce (400g) can of chopped tomatoes** and a little salt. Simmer for 10 minutes.

Peel and grate **8 ounces (250g) each of parsnips** and **carrots**. Peel **a small onion** and shred it finely. Mix the onion with the grated roots and **2 tablespoons of all-purpose flour**, then lightly beat **an egg** and stir it in. Mix in the remaining half of the spice mix and squish the mixture into 6 to 8 shallow patties. Fry them in a shallow nonstick pan in **a little oil** over moderate heat till lightly crisp, then turn and continue cooking briefly. Serve with the spiced tomato sauce.

For 2, as a hearty meal. Crisp, spicy.

On the grill

I have a rectangular, ridged iron grill pan. It sits on top of the gas jets of the stove and is where I often cook my steaks, lamb chops, and boned chicken pieces. I brown slices of eggplant on there too, and green onions and young, skinny leeks. It produces clouds of smoke, which need an efficient kitchen fan if they are not to set off the smoke alarm. The food that comes from it is the most delicious of all: a little singed, sizzling, and glistening with oil and caramelized sugars. It is one of the most used items in my kitchen.

I try not to wash my grill pan very much, preferring to wipe it with paper towels. A wet grill pan will rust. A new one will stick. But as it gets older, the patina (a posh word for burned-on grease) protects the iron and the washing becomes less of a problem. Even then, it should be dried quickly and put away if it isn't to get rust patches. I also use the broiler in my oven. This produces a different effect, as the food doesn't directly touch the heat, but it has been the source of many a daily dinner.

Ideally, I would grill my food over charcoal. But that must be done outside, and I'm not about to go into battle with charcoal and matches after a day's work. It has to be said that a stove-top grill pan or a broiler will never quite produce the same flavor as when food is cooked over charcoal. Nevertheless, food grilled indoors can be pretty damned good. I like the direct heat of the stove-top grill—the charring, the smoke, the slightly primitive flavors that ensue.

This grill chapter is short and sweet: some chops, a couple of ideas for chicken, and a pork chop. Yet these are the recipes I probably use most during the week. Grilled meat, a bowl of salad, a glass of wine. Dinner, as good as it gets.

A few favorites

Sweet roast garlic, soft butter, French bread
Wrap a head of garlic in foil with a little oil and thyme and bake for 40 minutes or so. Squeeze the cloves out into a bowl and coarsely mash with a little butter and salt. Grill a couple of boned chicken legs and, when almost done, spread the surface of the meat with the roast garlic butter. Serve with a baguette, torn into rough, crackle-crusted chunks, on the side for mopping up the butter.

Scallops, fresh chile
Mix scallops with olive oil, finely chopped mild red chile, and a little coarse black pepper and leave to marinate for about half an hour. Thread them onto wooden skewers, alternating with large chunks of peeled and seeded cucumber. Grill and serve with arugula leaves, fresh cilantro, and lemon.

Berbere lamb. The mystery of long pepper, nigella, chile, and basil
Rub lamb chops with olive oil and dust with a purchased Berbere spice blend. Grill, then serve with a salad of orange and mint.

Grilled shrimp, garlic mayo

Peel, then crush a clove of garlic with a little salt, beat in 2 egg yolks and a squeeze of lemon juice, then slowly, drop by drop at first, whisk in ½ cup (125ml) peanut or sunflower oil and ½ cup (125ml) olive oil. Toss whole, raw, shell-on shrimp in a little peanut or sunflower oil, then grill till pink and sizzling. Serve with the garlic mayonnaise.

The ancient scent of za'atar and olives

Season lamb steaks or chops with olive oil, salt, and pepper. Halfway through grilling, dust with za'atar—the dry mix of thyme, savory, sumac, and sometimes sesame, sold in Middle Eastern grocer's shops—and add a little more olive oil. Continue grilling for a few minutes, taking care that the spice does not burn (its usual use is to season flatbreads). Scatter with green olives and finish with a squeeze of lemon.

Black garlic and olives. A breath of southwest France

Squeeze a head of the black garlic out of its skins and mix to a thick paste with a little olive oil. Stir in some finely chopped black olives and thyme leaves, then spread it over lamb chops or steaks and grill.

A few thoughts on the grilled chicken

I find the most satisfying way to grill chicken is to take a boned leg and cook it on a hot ridged grill. Boning a chicken leg is easy. A thigh even more so. Place the meat, plump side down, on a chopping board. Make two deep cuts with a small, sharp knife following the two bones. Wiggle the knife in and out, slicing the flesh away from the bones, until you have two clean bones and a rough rectangle of chicken flesh. Keep the skin on.

And some variations

Miso chicken—possibly my favorite fast-food recipe ever

There, I've said it. In a small saucepan, warm together 6 tablespoons of mirin, 2 tablespoons of white (shiro) miso, and a little oil. Toss the boned chicken thighs in the mixture, making sure they are well coated, then cook under the broiler, basting regularly, till the skin is golden and crisp.

Chicken with thyme, sea salt, butter, lemon

Melt butter and add chopped fresh thyme leaves. Grill the boned and flattened chicken leg as in the recipe opposite. As the chicken grills, brush it with the butter. Once the chicken is golden on both sides and the skin a little crisp, scatter with sea salt flakes and finish with a generous squeeze of lemon.

Dark soy and golden honey, chile fire

Stir a very finely chopped hot red chile into an equal mixture of dark soy sauce and honey and brush this over the chicken as it grills. Offer halved limes at the table.

Citrus Chile Grilled Chicken

chicken legs, lime, lemon, red pepper flakes

Remove the bones from **2 chicken legs** with a small, sharp knife, then place each rectangle of meat on a piece of plastic wrap, fold the wrap over the meat, and pound with a rolling pin so it increases by half of its original size.

Make several narrow slits through the skin and the meat with the point of a sharp knife, going about halfway through the meat. Rub a scant teaspoon of sea salt flakes into the skin and down into the cuts. Grate the **zest of a lime** and the **zest of a lemon**, rub them into the skin, then do the same with **a large pinch of crumbled red pepper flakes**.

Place the chicken, skin side up, under a broiler, adding **a little oil** only if it looks a little dry, and cook for 6 to 9 minutes, till sizzling and golden.

Squeeze **the juice of the lime** and **the juice of the lemon** on top, season generously with sea salt, and eat immediately. Soft bread and butter. A rice pilaf maybe.

For 2. Feisty chicken.

Grilled Lamb
with Minted Feta

lamb chops, feta, mint, yogurt, garlic

Put **6 tablespoons of olive oil** in a shallow dish, then peel and crush
a clove of garlic and stir it into the olive oil with a grinding of salt
and pepper. Put **6 lamb chops** into the olive oil and turn them over to
cover them with the oil. Leave in a cool place for an hour or longer.

To make the minted feta, put **7 ounces (200g) feta cheese** into a
food processor and process briefly. Add **4 tablespoons of yogurt,
10 or so mint leaves**, and a few twists of black pepper, then puree
again for a few seconds, till you have a thick cream. Scoop into a bowl
with a rubber spatula and refrigerate till needed.

Cook the chops under the broiler or on a hot grill till the outside is
golden brown, the bones a little charred, and the inside rose pink.
Remove the chops from the broiler or grill and place on warm plates
with large spoonfuls of the feta cream.

For 2. Forks not required.

A few thoughts on the chicken wings

- *Umeboshi* plums are expensive and not something you will find at the corner shop, but I love this little recipe. Gourmet grocers and Japanese food stores are good places to look for them. Make no mistake, these plums are unrelentingly salty and sour, and you will not want to add any salt to the chutney. Start with a small amount of sugar and increase it to your taste, but don't lose the salty-sourness.
- Cook the onions down slowly so that they are really sweet and soft before you add the umeboshi. The longer and slower the better.
- This would make a good glaze for pork ribs too.

Chicken Wings with Onion Umeboshi Chutney

chicken wings, onion, umeboshi plums, sugar

Peel and slice **a large onion**, then let it soften in **a tablespoon of peanut or canola oil** in a shallow pan over moderate heat. While it is cooking, remove and discard the pits from **7 ounces (200g) umeboshi plums** and chop the flesh.

When the onion has started to turn a honey color, add the umeboshi and ½ **cup (100ml) water**. Continue cooking for 10 minutes, then sweeten a little with **sugar** to taste. Start with a teaspoon and continue till the sauce is salty, sour, and sweet. Simmer down till thick and gloopy. Turn off the heat and set aside.

In **a little oil**, fry **12 large free-range chicken wings** till golden all over, then add them to the plum and onion mixture and stir them so that they are lightly coated.

Preheat the broiler or a grill. Broil or grill the wings, with a little sauce adhering to them, till lightly crisp and golden brown. Serve with the remaining umeboshi and onion mixture to dip.

For 2 to 3. Salty, fruity, curiously addictive.

A note on the pork chops

Long pepper is a softly aromatic pepper-like spice available at spice shops and some Asian groceries.

And a few variations

Sweet and garlicky

Stew thinly sliced red peppers, fresh or from a can, in olive oil with thinly sliced red onion and garlic. The longer you cook it, the sweeter and stickier it becomes. Finish with basil and serve with the chops.

Pear, walnut, shallot, vermouth

Peel a large shallot, halve lengthwise, and unfurl, then cook in butter in a shallow pan. Cut a pear into thick slices and, as the shallots soften, add to the pan, then add a few thinner slices of pear so they break down into a slush as they cook. Toss in a few walnuts. Lastly, pour in a splash of dry vermouth. Cook for 5 minutes more, then serve with the chops.

A savory side

Fry a chopped shallot in olive oil, add a little chopped anchovy, and let it break down, then add thinly sliced button mushrooms and chopped parsley.

Pork Chop with Plum Chutney

pork chops, plums, onion, juniper
berries, cloves, sugar, long pepper,
red wine vinegar

Peel, halve, and slice **a large onion** into thick segments. Remove and
discard the pits from **1 pound (500g) plums**. Put the onion and plums
in a deep pan and add **4 crushed juniper berries, 2 cloves, 3 tablespoons
of superfine sugar, 2 tails of long pepper**, and a generous grinding of
salt. Simmer over low to moderate heat for about 15 minutes, then
add **3 tablespoons of red wine vinegar** and check the seasoning. Grill
4 pork chops and serve with the warm chutney.

For 4. Sweet meat, pickled plum.

A few thoughts on the lamb chops

- Small lamb chops do not need to marinate for long—15 minutes or so will do.
- Choose quite lean chops to avoid too much smoke when grilling.
- Let the bones brown and even char a little; they are good to pick up and eat.
- Use thick coconut cream in cans. You can also use the cream scooped off the top of a can of coconut milk.

A pork version

Pork, cut into thick finger-like strips, can be substituted for the lamb. Add about a teaspoon of cumin seeds to the spices. Include a little chopped green onion or finely chopped shallot. Use thick yogurt instead of the coconut cream. Serve with coarsely chopped cilantro.

Lamb Chops with Mustard Seed and Coconut

lamb chops, coconut cream, ground
coriander, black mustard seeds, garlic,
ginger, cabbage

Spoon ⅔ **cup (160ml) coconut cream** into a shallow bowl. Add
**2 teaspoons of ground coriander, 2 tablespoons of black mustard
seeds**, and a grinding of black pepper. Peel **2 cloves of garlic** and
chop finely. Peel **a thumb-size piece of fresh ginger** and shred
it, matchstick style, then stir both the garlic and ginger into the
coconut cream. Roll **6 lamb chops** in the coconut cream and leave
for 15 minutes.

　　Heat a grill pan or broiler and cook the chops till lightly golden
brown. Expect quite a bit of smoke. Shred **10 ounces (300g) Savoy or
other dark-leaved cabbage**, then fry quickly in **a little butter or oil**.

　　For 2. Sizzling chops.

A thought on the kippers

Golden beets seem less sweet to me than the more common red varieties, but it could just be my imagination. Either is suitable for mashing. The heat of the fresh horseradish is pleasing with the sweet earthiness of the beets.

And a few variations

Panfried haddock, parsley sauce, olive oil, and lemon mash

A parsley sauce for panfried haddock, made by simply adding crème fraîche to the pan once the fish is cooked along with a handful of finely chopped spanking-fresh parsley and simmering for a minute or two. Serve with a loose mash made from waxy potatoes, olive oil, and lemon juice (add the lemon juice to the olive oil before mixing with the potatoes).

Smoked haddock, bacon, cabbage mash

Grill or bake the smoked haddock. Cook the bacon, then make a mash with coarsely chopped cabbage and potatoes.

Salmon, creamed green peas

Boil and drain shelled green peas, then blitz them to a puree with butter and a few leaves of mint. Serve with baked or grilled salmon.

Grilled Kippers, Beets, and Horseradish Mash

kippers, beets, fresh horseradish, butter

Scrub but do not peel **4 medium-size red or golden beets**, then boil them whole in a pot of lightly salted water for 30 minutes or so, depending on their size. They must be truly tender. Skin them—you should be able to slide the skin off with your thumb—then trim them neatly before returning them to the pan and crushing with a potato masher. Beat in **3½ tablespoons (50g) butter** with a wooden spoon, seasoning with salt and **2 tablespoons of grated fresh horseradish**.

While the beets are cooking, get a grill or grill pan hot, then lightly brush **2 kippers or 4 fillets** with **oil** and cook for 3 or 4 minutes on each side. Alternatively, cook them in a shallow pan with **a little butter**. Serve alongside the beet and horseradish mash.

For 2. Smoky fish, sweet beets, hot horseradish.

Couscous, Lemons,
Almonds, Squid

couscous, lemon, preserved lemon, Marcona almonds, squid, green olives, lime, parsley

Plump up ⅔ **cup (125g) couscous** in 1⅓ cups (325ml) freshly boiled water or stock into which you have squeezed the juice of **a lemon**. Add the empty lemon halves to the couscous for flavor. Chop **a preserved lemon** into tiny dice, discarding its pulp. Mix with **a handful of toasted salted Marcona almonds, a handful of pitted green olives, a little lime juice**, and **lots of chopped flat-leaf parsley** and add to the couscous. Finish with black pepper and just a shake of **very fruity olive oil**.

Score **1 pound (500g) prepared squid** lightly with a sharp knife, then cut into large pieces. Grill for a couple of minutes, till lightly cooked, the surface a little charred here and there. Place on the couscous.

For 2. Warm grains of couscous. Grilled seafood. A spritz of lemon.

On the stove

My first apartment had no oven, only a hot plate on which to cook dinner. Pretty good some of them were too: little vegetable curries, lamb stews, sautéed chicken, and endless, endless pasta suppers. Dishes cooked on the stove, in a high-sided frying pan or deeper saucepan, are generally things that take longer than the frying-pan dinners of the earlier chapter. The deeper pans allow you to cook in liquid and in larger quantities. You can boil fettuccine or simmer meat in a sauce; steam basmati or stir a soup.

For the most part, these are dishes cooked in a single pot that will sit over gas or electric heat at a rolling boil, a calm simmer, or quietly plodding toward tenderness. Most require a lid of some sort. We are talking fried chicken with bread sauce, slow sautés with their pan juices, clams cooked in their own steam. And then there's pasta, of course: tangles of *pappardelle* and little pasta shapes that hold a sauce; there is couscous, lentils, and beans.

We cover food with a lid to keep its liquid from evaporating, to allow it to cook a little more slowly than in a shallow open pan, giving it time to cook right through to its heart. We often start by browning the surface of the food lightly, then adding liquid before covering it with a lid. Not all my pans have a lid. I have to use a plate sometimes.

A lid also permits the food to cook in its own steam. Mussels and clams, perhaps, things that produce their own juices and take just seconds to cook. We trap in the steam they produce, encouraging them to cook more quickly. Sometimes, the lid is on tight, so no steam escapes; other times it is left at a jaunty angle, like a cap.

I have an assortment of pans, some of which have been around as long as my oldest friends: a cast-iron pan whose thick bottom allows a lump of meat to cook evenly; a set of stainless steel pans that I have had for two decades (the best money I have ever spent); a copper-based sauté pan with curved edges and a lid, for cooking chicken pieces; and a vast pan with tall sides that gives room for pasta to roll around in deep boiling water. Not many, I concede, but that is generally all I need.

Cooking on the stove is often about heat control—the first burst of heat to form a crust, then a lower heat to cook the meat, fish, or vegetable right through to the middle. If we turn the heat down really low, or use a diffuser, then the food can be left unattended. Generally, anything cooked on the stove needs watching, even if it is only to give it the occasional stir. I have burned many a pot of soup by being distracted.

I tend to think of the stove as the home of the cheap dinner. Less expensive to heat than the oven, the stove is where we can make a bowl of pasta, a hearty main-course soup, a noodle broth, or a vast pan of mussels. This is the place I boil lentils for a bolognaise, poach a chicken for salad, or cook up a mound of mash for sausages. What I like about cooking on the stove is that I can stir to my heart's content. Unlike opening the oven door, grabbing a tea towel, and sliding out the baking dish, you simply have to lift the lid and you are immediately in touch with your food. This is the food whose smell fills our kitchen as we cook. It brings us to the table. The joy of stirring a dish while we drink and chat with those we are feeding. Cooking on the stove allows us to get closer to our cooking than roasting or baking does. It allows us a sniff, a peep, a stir, a taste. The very best sort of hands-on cooking.

A few favorite stove-top dinners

Cannellini mash, butter, and spices, warm naan
Warm and mash cannellini or navy beans. Toast some whole cumin seed, ground coriander, and ground chile in a pan till fragrant, then add to the beans. Stir a little melted butter into the bean mash, then scoop up with warm naan bread. Or serve in a soft mound alongside grilled ham or grilled lamb chops.

A chicken stroganoff, of sorts
Cut dark and white chicken meat into rough chunks (about the size of a walnut in its shell), then roll them in a mixture of ground paprika, salt, and pepper. Heat a little butter and oil in a shallow pan, add a sliced onion, and let it soften. Add a handful of quartered small mushrooms and let both lightly brown, then transfer to a bowl. Add a little more butter to the pan. When it froths, add the chicken and let it color. Add the onion and mushroom in with the chicken, stir in a generous seasoning of Dijon mustard, salt, and pepper, then add a container of crème fraîche. Simmer for 6 to 7 minutes. Eat with noodles, bread, or rice.

A few thoughts on the beans

- You could spread the bean mixture on bruschetta or crispbread and place the crisp bacon, cut into short lengths, on top.
- Once you have rinsed the beans, you can cook them in water or a little olive oil, depending how rich you want the mash to be.
- Canned butter beans and cannellini seem to make the smoothest mash. Chickpeas produce a slightly grainy texture.
- If you drain a can of beans, warm them in a little olive oil, and then puree to a smooth mash, you have an instant dip for scooping up with chunks of torn baguette or toasted sourdough.

And a couple of variations

Creamed beans, garlic bread, olive oil

Drain a couple of cans of butter beans, chickpeas, or cannellini beans, rinse them in a colander under cold running water, then put them in a saucepan with a can of water and bring to a boil. Lower the heat and simmer for 10 minutes to heat thoroughly, then drain. Mash with a potato masher or fork, or in a food processor, beating in a couple of tablespoons of olive oil and seasoning with salt, black pepper, and lemon juice. Mash a clove of garlic with a little butter, spread it on hot toast or a halved baguette, then spread generously with the bean mash. Drizzle over some more olive oil, perhaps something rich and fruity.

Flageolet, green herbs, olive oil

Rinse a couple of cans of flageolet (or cannellini) beans, put them in a saucepan with 2 tablespoons of olive oil and some salt and pepper, and warm them for a few minutes. Coarsely mash the beans with a fork or potato masher, then pile onto slices of toasted baguette and scatter with chopped parsley, basil, and a few capers. Drizzle over a little olive oil and finish with a grinding of pepper.

Bacon and Beans

bacon, chickpeas, butter beans, onion, garlic, paprika, crème fraîche

Peel **a medium onion** and coarsely chop it. Warm **a film of olive oil** in a deep frying pan and soften the onion in it over moderate heat. Peel and crush **a large clove of garlic** and add to the pan. Drain **a 14-ounce (400g) can of chickpeas** and **a 14-ounce (400g) can of butter beans** and rinse briefly in a colander under running water. Put them in a pan with **2 tablespoons of oil** and heat for 5 minutes to warm thoroughly. Add to the cooked onion.

Season the onion and beans with **a little ground paprika** and some salt and black pepper. Puree in a food processor, then stir in **a couple of tablespoons of crème fraîche**. Broil or fry **8 slices of bacon** till thoroughly crisp. Serve with the bean puree.

For 2, as a light meal. The soft earthiness of mashed beans. The warmth of spice. Crisp bacon.

Chicken Skin Popcorn

chicken skin, popcorn, butter, rosemary

Preheat the oven to 350°F (180°C). Remove the skin from **4 free-range chicken thighs** with a small knife, place it flat on a baking sheet, then lightly season with coarse sea salt and black pepper. Bake for 20 to 25 minutes, till crisp and golden. Remove from the oven and place on paper towels to fully crisp.

Melt **3½ tablespoons (50g) butter** in a small pan, add **a heaping tablespoon of rosemary needles**, very finely chopped, and cook very briefly till fragrant.

Crumble the chicken skin into small pieces and season generously with sea salt. (Only you know how salty you like your popcorn, but start with half a tablespoon of sea salt flakes.)

Melt **another 2 tablespoons (30g) butter** in a deep pan. Add **¾ cup (150g) popcorn** and cover with a lid. Over medium heat, cook the corn till it starts to pop, shaking the pan vigorously from time to time to ensure it doesn't scorch.

As soon as all the corn has popped—there may be a few stubborn kernels that refuse—pour in the melted rosemary butter and add the crumbled chicken skin.

For 4, as a snack. Scandalously salty, moreish popcorn.

A thought on the chorizo

I use a thick, semisoft chorizo for this. A firm one might need to be quite thinly sliced to keep it from becoming chewy during its short time in the pan. I also go for a hot one, so good with the clam juices, but there are plenty of mild chorizos around if you prefer. *Picante* is the spicy one, *dulce* the sweeter.

Some ideas for shellfish and pork

Sweet mussels, crisp smoked bacon

Cut 7 ounces (200g) bacon into large dice and fry it in a shallow pan. As it starts to crisp and the fat turns amber, add 1½ pounds (750g) small, sweet mussels in their shells. Toss together, allowing the bacon and mussel juices to mix. Add a glass of dry vermouth, such as Noilly Prat, and a handful of chopped flat-leaf parsley.

Mackerel wrapped in bacon

Season fillets of fresh mackerel with black pepper and twist a slice, or even two, of bacon around each one. Cook under a broiler till the mackerel is tender and the bacon is crisp. Eat with a salad of thinly sliced fennel, dill, and lemon juice.

Pancetta, salmon, crisp baguette

Cut thin slices of pancetta into postage-stamp-size pieces and fry in a nonstick pan for a couple of minutes. Add chunks of cold cooked salmon and leave to cook, with the occasional shake of the pan to stop them from sticking. Try not to let the salmon break up. Split pieces of crisp baguette open and slather with mayonnaise. Pile the salmon and pancetta on top of the mayo and squeeze over a little lemon juice.

Mussels with Clams and Chorizo

mussels, clams, chorizo, dry sherry

Wash **1 pound (500g) mussels** and **1 pound (500g) clams**, discarding any with cracked or broken shells, any that seem lifeless or exceptionally light, and any open ones that refuse to close when tapped on the side of the kitchen sink. Tug off any wiry beards from the mussels and knock off any barnacles with the back of a knife.

Remove the casing from **7 ounces (200g) fresh chorizo** and slice or tear it into small chunks. Get a wok or deep frying pan very hot, add **a tablespoon of oil**, then add the chorizo and let it color lightly, tossing it around the pan so it doesn't burn. Pour in **a glass of dry sherry** and let it boil briefly (you need the flavor, not the alcohol), then put the washed mussels and clams into the pan and let them cook for a minute or two, till the shells open, discarding any that stubbornly refuse to open. Season lightly.

Serve immediately, with the juices and some bread for mopping them up.

For 2. Shellfish, sherry, and sausages.

On the side of the lentils

Any ribbon pasta will be fine for serving with the lentil ragù, as will almost any smaller shape that will hold some sauce, especially orecchiette.

And a few variations

Lentils and golden onions, smoked bacon, crème fraîche

Cook Puy lentils in boiling water until tender and then drain. Cook a thinly sliced onion in a little olive oil or butter till pale gold, then add 4 slices chopped bacon and cook till they are sizzling and the onion is a rich golden color. Stir in the drained lentils, some coarsely chopped parsley, and a couple of tablespoons of crème fraîche. Eat with steamed brown rice, with pasta, or as a side dish.

Lentils, green peas, and grilled salmon

Boil Puy lentils, drain them, and toss with warm cooked fava beans, popped from their gray skins, some cooked peas, and finely sliced green onions. Stir into them a generous glug or two of olive oil, then add large pieces of crumbled grilled salmon. Maybe serve as a side dish.

Goat cheese, lentils, olive oil

Simmer Puy lentils in vegetable stock until tender, then drain. Toss with a little olive oil, salt, and pepper. Serve warm, topped with thick slices cut from a log of soft goat cheese, such as Tymsboro, Ragstone, or Dorstone. Or use the cooked lentils as a base on which to pile feta cheese that you have baked in foil with thyme leaves and a little olive oil.

Lentil Bolognaise

Puy lentils, carrots, onion, vegetable stock, crème fraîche, balsamic vinegar, pappardelle

Cut **2 carrots** into small dice, peeling them if you wish, then leave them to cook over moderate heat in **3 tablespoons of olive oil** in a deep pan. Peel and finely slice **an onion**, add to the pan, and cook for a good 15 minutes, till the onion is deep gold and the carrots lightly browned.

Add **1 cup (200g) Puy lentils**, rinsed if necessary, into the pan, then pour in **4 cups (1 liter) of vegetable stock** and bring to a boil. Lower the heat so the liquid simmers and leave to cook until the lentils are soft—anything from 25 to 40 minutes. Season with salt toward the end of cooking.

Put a large pan of water on to boil for the pasta and salt it generously. Cook **10 ounces (300g) pappardelle** in it until al dente.

While the pasta cooks, remove half the lentils and their liquid and process to a coarse puree in a blender or food processor. Return them to the pan and stir. Mix in **2 tablespoons of crème fraîche** and **a tablespoon of balsamic vinegar** and check the seasoning. Bring almost to a boil.

Drain the pasta, divide among warm bowls, then spoon over the lentil ragù.

For 4. Earthy, frugal, and filling.

A few changes to the orecchiette

Chopped tarragon, mint, and chervil are appropriate herbs to add. A scattering of grated Parmesan, tiny nuggets of pecorino, or shavings of aged ricotta will add a savory hit. Shelled peas or snow peas will bring more sweetness, just as sliced button mushrooms cooked in a little butter will introduce an earthiness. The recipe is a gentle one, so it is not worth adding anything too robust or powerful.

Other delicate summer flavors for pasta

- Fold lightly cooked green beans into cooked ribbon pasta with some crème fraîche, Parmesan, and a little grated lemon zest.
- Warm heavy cream in a small pan, add black pepper, flaked cooked salmon, and chopped dill. Toss with pasta.
- Boil and drain shelled or frozen peas, toss them with small pasta, watercress, basil, and warmed crème fraîche.
- Drain marinated artichoke hearts from their oil, slice them, then warm with torn parsley, lemon juice, and shredded Parma ham. Toss with any ribbon pasta.
- Chop a couple of handfuls of mixed fresh herbs—basil, tarragon, dill, parsley, chives. Mash them into softened butter with a little salt and black pepper. Drain the cooked pasta—ribbons of fettuccine or pappardelle would be appropriate—then toss with the soft, but not melted, butter.

Orecchiette with Ricotta and Fava Beans

orecchiette, ricotta, fava beans

Drop **14 ounces (400g) fava beans** into boiling, lightly salted water, cook for 7 to 8 minutes, depending on their size, then drain in a colander. Cook **8 ounces (250g) orecchiette or other medium-size pasta** in deep, generously salted boiling water until al dente. While the pasta is cooking, squeeze the beans from their gray skins. Discard the skins and toss the beans in **a splash of olive oil**.

Drain the pasta, transfer to a large bowl, then add the fava beans. Stir **a couple of tablespoons of olive oil** into **¾ cup (200g) ricotta**— there may be a little curdling—and season with black pepper. Drop large spoonfuls of the ricotta on top of the pasta and serve.

For 3. Delicate flavors. The marriage of warm and cool.

A few variations on the chicken ragù

Liver and bacon ragù. Amazing depth from a ragù so quickly cooked. The richness of liver

Dice 8 thick slices of bacon and cook over low to moderate heat in a nonstick pan. Peel and dice a red onion. As the bacon fat starts to run, add the onion to the pan and cook for 5 minutes. Finely chop 6 cremini mushrooms, stir them into the bacon and onion, and continue cooking till the mushrooms are glossy and tender. Push everything to one side of the pan, add 8 ounces (250g) lamb's liver, chopped into small dice, and cook for 2 to 3 minutes. Cut 12 cherry tomatoes into quarters and stir them in. Let the tomatoes cook down for a few minutes, then add a wineglass or so of stock. Leave to simmer for 5 to 10 minutes, scraping up any goodies stuck to the bottom of the pan into the sauce, until the sauce has reduced a little—it won't thicken a great deal.

Cook 4 ounces (125g) fettuccine in generously salted boiling water. Drain the pasta and toss gently with the sauce.

A vegetable version. Ragù of leek and Caerphilly

Trim 2 large leeks and slice them lengthwise into long, thin ribbons, like pappardelle. Cook them slowly in butter, without letting them color, till they are soft. Add a couple of cloves of finely sliced garlic, a tablespoon of chopped tarragon, a little heavy cream, and 5 ounces (150g) deeply flavored, crumbled farmhouse Caerphilly. Toss with cooked ribbon pasta. Shave a further 3½ ounces (100g) Caerphilly or so on top.

A Light Chicken Ragù

chicken, garlic, green onion, lemon thyme, parsley, lemon, chicken stock, pappardelle or fettuccine

Cut **14 ounces (400g) boned chicken breast** into very small dice, just a step or two up from mince. Peel and thinly slice **2 cloves of garlic** and thinly slice **a green onion**. Lightly brown the chicken in **a little oil or butter**. As the color turns, add the garlic and green onion. Stir in **a tablespoon of lemon thyme, 2 tablespoons of chopped parsley**, some salt and pepper, then **2 tablespoons of all-purpose flour**. Cook for a minute or two, then pour in **1²/₃ cups (400ml) hot chicken stock**. Simmer for 15 minutes, stirring regularly. Check the seasoning and finish with **a squeeze of lemon**.

Cook **4 ounces (125g) pappardelle or fettuccine** in a large pot of generously salted water, then drain and toss with the ragù sauce.

For 2. Light, creamy, and fresh. A change from a dark ragù sauce.

A few variations on the chicken and spelt

With prosciutto, crème fraîche, and tarragon

Sauté 2 large boneless chicken breasts in a little olive oil over low
to moderate heat, turning them regularly and basting them as they
cook. Remove them from the pan as soon as their juices run clear
when you pierce the meat with a skewer at the thickest part. Tear
4 thin slices of prosciutto into pieces and coarsely chop a handful
of tarragon leaves. Add a little butter to the pan, followed by the
prosciutto and tarragon, then stir in a couple of tablespoons of crème
fraîche and return the chicken and any juices to the pan. Green beans
would be good with this. For 2.

With tomato sauce and mozzarella

Slice a couple of cloves of garlic, warm them in olive oil, then add a can
of chopped tomatoes, a handful of torn basil leaves, and a little salt and
black pepper. Simmer for 6 to 7 minutes. Brown 4 chicken breasts in a
little oil, then place in a baking dish, pour over the tomato and basil
sauce, and lay thick slices of mozzarella on top. Scatter a layer of grated
Parmesan on top and bake for 25 minutes at 350°F (180°C). For 4.

Chicken, earthy spice, sweet sharp apricots

Brown 6 chicken thighs in oil in a deep pan, then add a peeled and
finely sliced onion and a couple of sliced cloves of garlic, followed
by 2 tablespoons of ras el hanout. Add a handful of dried apricots,
2 chopped tomatoes, and 3⅓ cups (800ml) chicken stock. Bring to
a boil, season, and cover with a lid, then simmer gently for a good
hour. For 3.

Ras el Hanout
Chicken and Spelt

chicken wings, pearled spelt, ras el hanout,
cabbage, butter

Fry **8 chicken wings** in **3 tablespoons of oil** in a Dutch oven. When
they start to brown, stir in **2 tablespoons of ras el hanout**. Add
a rounded 1 cup (200g) pearled spelt and pour in **1²/₃ cups (400ml)
boiling water**. Bring back to a boil, lid on, then transfer to an oven
heated to 350°F (180°C) and bake for 35 to 40 minutes, till the liquid
has been absorbed.

Shred **4 cabbage leaves**, add them to the mixture with **2 tablespoons
(30g) butter**, and cook briefly on the stove before serving.

Enough for 2 to 3. Tender grains. The warmth of Moroccan spice.

A couple of variations on the haddock

Smoked haddock, the cosseting of mushrooms and cream

Thinly slice a handful of button mushrooms and cook them in
a shallow nonstick pan with a little butter till they are soft and
lightly colored. Stir in a drained and rinsed 14-ounce (400g) can of
cannellini beans and warm through, stirring from time to time. Put
a couple of pieces of smoked haddock fillet, about 7 ounces (200g)
each, into a second pan, with 1⅔ cups (400ml) heavy cream. Add a
couple of bay leaves and 6 black peppercorns and simmer gently for
about 12 minutes, until the fish is tender. Lift the fish out onto plates.
Pour the cream through a sieve onto the beans and mushrooms,
cook briefly (some chopped parsley would be good, if you have it),
then spoon the mixture over the fish.

Kippers, butter beans, and cream

Put a couple of kipper fillets in a shallow pan. Pour over enough heavy
cream just to cover them, add 6 black peppercorns and a bay leaf, and
bring to a boil. Immediately turn down the heat. Let the cream simmer
gently for 10 minutes, then turn off the heat. Cover the pan with a plate
and give the cream 10 minutes more to infuse with smoke from the
kippers, bay, and pepper. Empty a 14-ounce (400g) can of butter beans
into a sieve and rinse them under cold running water. Break the fish
into large bite-size pieces, removing the bones as you go. Warm the
beans over moderate heat with enough of the cream to cover them.
Add the pieces of kipper, a little salt, lemon juice, and, if you like, a
grating of horseradish.

Smoked Haddock with Lentils

smoked haddock, green lentils, carrots, onion, vegetable stock, heavy cream, parsley, bay, black peppercorns

Put **1 cup (250ml) heavy cream** in a shallow pan. Remove the skin from **a piece of smoked haddock weighing about 12 ounces (350g)** and add the haddock to the pan. Add **6 black peppercorns** and **3 bay leaves**, bring to a boil, then turn off the heat and cover with a lid. The fish will cook in the residual heat.

Finely dice **a couple of medium carrots** and **an onion**. Cook them in **a thick slice of butter** over moderate heat for 5 minutes, then add **¾ cup (150g) green lentils** and **1⅔ cups (400ml) vegetable stock**. Bring to a boil and turn the heat down to a simmer. Leave to cook for 20 minutes, till the lentils are approaching softness, then stir in the cream from the fish. Continue cooking, letting the liquid reduce until it just covers the lentils.

Add **a good handful of chopped parsley** and season carefully with salt and pepper. Divide between 2 dishes, putting the haddock on top of the lentils.

For 2. The calming quality of smoked fish and cream.

A thought on the mackerel

Whole smoked mackerel is moister and has creamier flesh than the fillets. But use whatever you can. I like to keep the pieces of fish large and heat them gently in the cream with as little stirring as possible, so as not to crush them.

For a change

- The cream can be infused with other flavors, such as a few sprigs of thyme or a tablespoon or two of chopped dill, tarragon, or chervil. Mustard is a fine addition, especially the grainy sort. A little lemon is good too.
- You could add lightly sautéed strips of zucchini in place of the green beans in the recipe opposite.

Green spinach, smoked mackerel, ribbons of pasta

Cook the mackerel in the cream as opposite. Boil enough pappardelle for 2 in a large pot of salted water. Wash 4 handfuls of spinach and, without shaking them dry, put them into a pan with a lid. Cover and let the leaves steam briefly till they have just wilted, then drain in a colander and rinse under cold running water. Squeeze dry with your hands, then tuck bits of spinach between ribbons of pasta and shards of torn smoked mackerel. Pour the seasoned cream on top.

Chewy, glossy bagel. Creamy smoked fish

Break a smoked mackerel fillet into pieces, mash it coarsely with a fork, then fold in a little whole-grain mustard, black pepper, and cream. Spread it onto bagels, with or without slices of cucumber.

Smoked Mackerel and Green Beans

smoked mackerel, green beans, heavy cream, bay, parsley

Pour **2 cups (450ml) heavy cream** into a saucepan, season with coarsely ground black pepper, and add **a couple of bay leaves**. Place over moderate heat. Once the cream is almost at a boil, break **12 ounces (350g) smoked mackerel** into large pieces and drop into the cream. Simmer for a couple of minutes, then turn off the heat. During this time the cream will soak up the smoky flavors of the mackerel.

Top and tail **8 ounces (250g) green beans** and blanch them in salted water. Drain the beans and toss with the cream and mackerel. Warm gently, season thoughtfully, and serve with **a little chopped parsley**.

Enough for 2. The ever-useful smoked mackerel.

A couple thoughts on the scrambled eggs

- Basically Spanish-inspired scrambled eggs, this is a dish to which you could add cooked shrimp, bacon, or ham, or chopped cooked greens such as spinach or summer cabbage.
- Chopped or quartered mushrooms can be added to the pan before the spice paste, as can morcilla (blood sausage), peppers, chorizo, or slices of squid. It is very much a recipe for last-minute inspiration.

Some variations

Asparagus and shrimp

Sizzle butter in a pan, drop in some shavings of asparagus (I use a vegetable peeler), let them soften for a minute, then add a handful of shrimp. As soon as they are hot, stir in the eggs.

A salsa scramble

Sizzle a finely chopped tomato, a little finely chopped chile, and some chopped green onion in a little butter, then stir in half a chopped avocado, a squeeze of lime juice, and a little cilantro. Use half as the base of the scramble, adding the eggs to it once it is hot. Serve the other half as a salsa on the side.

A bacon scramble

Sizzle chopped bacon in butter, then add a handful of croutons and fry till crisp. Pour in lightly beaten eggs, add a handful of chopped parsley, and scramble as opposite.

Spinach and Parmesan

Steam a couple of large handfuls of spinach and chop coarsely, then stir into the beaten eggs together with finely ground black pepper and a couple of tablespoons of Parmesan or grana padano cheese. Add to the melted butter, stirring as opposite to give a loose scramble.

Spiced Scrambled Eggs

eggs, curry powder, cumin seeds, red pepper flakes, tomato, green onions, cilantro

In a food processor, puree **a large tomato** with **a teaspoon each of decent curry powder, cumin seeds**, and **red pepper flakes**. Put the resulting paste into a shallow pan with **a little butter** and fry gently over moderate heat for 4 or 5 minutes, stirring regularly. Finely slice **2 green onions** and add them to the spice paste. Break **5 eggs** straight into the pan and stir quickly so that they scramble and mix with the spiced tomato paste, then add **a little cilantro**. This dish is all about speed, so make it quickly and get everyone to the table first. It needs to be eaten fresh from the pan. For 2.

A couple of variations on the pasta

Gorgonzola, pasta, a little olive oil

Cook any pasta in a large pot of generously salted water. Warm ripe
Gorgonzola in a small bowl over hot water and stir in a little cream
and olive oil. Drain the pasta, then toss with the melted cheese sauce.

Zucchini and lemon pasta

Dice a couple of medium-size zucchini, then cook the cubes in butter
in a shallow pan till they are tender and golden. Finely chop 2 large
garlic cloves and let them color with the zucchini. Add a handful of
chopped mint leaves, a little grated lemon zest, and a little more
butter. Cook enough small pasta, such as penne or rigatoni, for 2 in a
large pot of salted water, drain, and toss with the zucchini and lemon.

Basil Tomato Pasta

basil, tomatoes, pasta, olive oil

Cook **5 ounces (150g) conchiglie or other pasta** in a large pot of salted water till just tender. Make a dressing by putting **⅔ cup (150ml) olive oil, 1 cup (20g) basil leaves, a beefsteak tomato**, and a little salt and pepper into a food processor or blender and processing till you have a coarse puree. Drain the pasta and return to the pan, then add the dressing and toss gently.

For 2. Hot pasta. Cold, fragrant dressing.

A few thoughts on the colcannon

- Colcannon, an Irish recipe from the bubble and squeak family, is traditionally served unfried, with kale, potatoes, and milk as the main ingredients. Often eaten with boiled ham, it can be a sound use for leftover ham too, which can be torn up and mixed with the mashed potato, as opposite.
- Wet potato will give a sloppy mash. Steaming the potatoes in their skins instead of boiling them is a successful way to get a dry, fluffy mash.
- For extra-light mashed potatoes, whip the mixture further after mashing, using a wooden spoon or an electric mixer.
- Use crème fraîche instead of milk, or add a handful of grated cheese.

For a change

Cheese and onion mash

In the colcannon recipe opposite, substitute green onions for the leeks. In place of ham, fold in cubes of Taleggio, Camembert, or other soft cheese, leaving it to soften in the warm potato. You will need about 3½ ounces (100g) cheese to 12 ounces (350g) of cooked potato.

Rumbledethumps, as robustly delicious as it sounds

Fry sliced onions in butter and a little oil till they are soft, deep gold, and glossy. This will take a good 20 minutes, if not longer. Stir them into the mashed potato with shredded cooked cabbage, then pile into a baking dish and brown lightly in the oven.

Bubble cakes

Take the colcannon opposite and pat the mixture into small cakes. Toss them lightly in flour, then fry in butter and oil till a crisp crust has appeared underneath. Turn them tenderly and cook the other side. Serve on their own or with a fried egg on top.

Ham and Kale Colcannon

ham, kale, potatoes, leeks, milk

Peel **1 pound (500g) large starchy potatoes**, cut them into large chunks, and cook in boiling water. Slice **8 ounces (250g) leeks** and fry in **butter** till soft but not colored. Steam **a couple of handfuls of kale** and drain. When the potatoes are soft enough to mash, drain, then beat to a fluff either with a potato masher and a wooden spoon or in a stand mixer. Beat in about ⅔ **cup (150ml) hot milk** and **a thick slice of butter**.

Tear up about **8 ounces (250g) thick-cut cooked ham**, chop the kale, and fold them into the potato together with the cooked leeks. Season with salt and black pepper and serve.

For 3 to 4. Comfort food of the highest order.

Mackerel with Bulgur
and Tomato

mackerel, bulgur, tomatoes, vegetable stock,
red wine vinegar

Heat 1²⁄₃ **cups (400ml) vegetable stock** in a saucepan, then pour it
over **1 cup (150g) bulgur wheat** and set aside for 15 minutes or so, until
most of the liquid has been absorbed by the grain.

Halve **8 medium-size tomatoes** and cook them under a broiler
till soft and the skins have started to blacken. Remove the skins, pour
in **a tablespoon of red wine vinegar**, and season with black pepper.
Crush the tomatoes with a fork to give a thick, coarsely textured sauce
and keep warm.

Brush **4 mackerel fillets** with **a little oil**, season with salt and
pepper, then cook under the broiler for a few minutes, skin side
down, till the fish is opaque and a flake will pull away from the skin.
I like to turn the fillets skin side up for a minute or so, to crisp them
lightly. Divide the bulgur between 2 plates, add the mackerel fillets,
then spoon over the broiled tomato sauce.

For 2. Homey grain. The sweet, sharp joy of tomatoes.

A few thoughts on the smoked haddock

- Use another type of fish if you prefer.
- You could peel the potatoes before cooking them and mash them to a soft cream for a more classic result.
- Include a little cooked spinach, well drained and squeezed dry, in place of the leeks.
- Add a few capers.
- Make a hollandaise to accompany.

For a change

Kipper, zucchini, dill

To the basic potato mixture opposite, add cooked and lightly crushed kippers (keep the pieces quite large) and some shredded zucchini that you have briefly fried with a little butter and dill. Fold into the potato mixture, shape, and fry.

Smoked Haddock and Leek Cakes

smoked haddock, leeks, potatoes, milk, bay, black peppercorns

Scrub **14 ounces (400g) russet or other starchy baking potatoes,** then cut into large chunks. Boil in a large pot of salted water for 10 to 15 minutes, till tender enough to mash. Drain the potatoes and crush them with a potato masher or a fork, keeping the texture rough and lumpy. Finely shred **14 ounces (400g) leeks**, then let them completely soften in **a thin slice of butter** over moderate heat.

Place **10 ounces (300g) smoked haddock, 1 cup (250ml) milk, a bay leaf**, and **6 black peppercorns** in a pan. Bring the milk to a boil, turn off the heat, cover with a lid, and leave for 10 minutes, until opaque (this is all the cooking it needs). When the fish is opaque, remove, discard the skin, and break the flesh into large flakes, then mix with the crushed potatoes and half the cooked leeks. Shape into 6 rough patties, then fry in **a little oil and butter** till crisp and golden and serve with the remaining leeks.

Makes 6. Enough for 3. A modern rough-textured take on the classic fish cake.

Shrimp, Linguine, Dill

shrimp, linguine, dill, garlic,
dry vermouth, lemon

Put a large pan of water on to boil, then salt it generously. When the water boils, add **7 ounces (200g) linguine**. Cook for the time given on the package, about 8 minutes.

Peel and crush **2 medium cloves of garlic**. Put **5 tablespoons of oil** in a small pan, add the garlic, and fry briefly till soft, then add **7 ounces (200g) raw brown or other small shrimp** and **a large handful of chopped dill**. Season with black pepper, salt, the **grated zest and juice of a lemon**, and **a tablespoon of Noilly Prat or other dry vermouth**. Bring to a boil, then remove from the heat.

Drain the linguine, add the shrimp mixture, and toss them gently together.

For 2. Light lunch. Summer flavors. The fun of little shrimp and dill.

A few thoughts on the minestrone

Chop and change the vegetables to suit what you have available. The point is to keep the ingredients fresh and green. French beans, chopped into short pieces, are an option, as is thickly shredded, mild-tasting spring cabbage.

To make the soup more substantial, you could add spaghetti, broken into short lengths, or any of the tiny star- or rice-shaped pastas. As this is a variation on the traditional tomato-based minestrone, there are no rules. You can add and subtract according to what is in your shopping bag. You could include some bits of chopped pancetta too. Cook them with the leeks and onions.

And a variation

A cream of cauliflower soup with mussels

Wash and thoroughly inspect 1¾ pounds (800g) mussels, discarding any that are open and refuse to close when tapped hard on the side of the sink or have broken shells. Put the mussels in a pan with 6 peppercorns, a couple of bay leaves, and ¾ cup (200ml) of water. Bring to a boil, cover with a lid, and steam for a couple of minutes, till all the shells have opened. Discard any that remain closed.

Remove the mussels from the pan, leaving the cooking liquid inside. Pick the mussels out of their shells and place in a bowl.

Break a medium cauliflower into large florets and steam over the mussel cooking liquid for 10 to 15 minutes, till tender, then strain the cooking liquid.

Toast 2 tablespoons of hazelnuts in a frying pan till golden. Puree the cauliflower and the strained mussel liquid in a blender or food processor till smooth. Stir in 1 cup (225ml) heavy cream, then check the seasoning and reheat if necessary (probably not). Add the shelled mussels, some chopped parsley, and the toasted hazelnuts. For 3 to 4.

A Quick(ish) Green Minestrone

fava beans, baby leeks, green onions,
zucchini, flageolet beans, peas, vegetable
stock, chives, parsley, Parmesan

Pod **14 ounces (400g) fava beans**, boil them in lightly salted water,
then drain and cool under running water. Unless they are really young
and small, I like to pop them out of their pale skins, but it is up to you.

Thickly slice **7 ounces (200g) leeks** (I like to do them diagonally), then
thinly slice **2 green onions**. Place them in a saucepan with **a couple of
tablespoons of olive oil** and cook gently, covered with a piece of waxed
paper or parchment. The parchment will encourage them to steam
and soften rather than fry. You want them to be tender, but they
shouldn't brown. Cut **7 ounces (200g) zucchini** into short lengths.

When the leeks and onions are soft and still bright green, remove
the paper, add the zucchini, **a 14-ounce (400g) can of flageolet beans**,
rinsed, and 1⅓ **cups (200g) shelled peas**. Add **4 cups (1 liter) of
vegetable stock**, bring to a boil, then turn down to a simmer. Add the
fava beans and **3 tablespoons chives**, in short lengths. Coarsely chop
a handful of parsley and stir into the soup. Season and pass round a
dish of **grated Parmesan** at the table. For 4 to 6.

A couple of variations on the chicken goujons

Black garlic and almonds

Squeeze the soft flesh from a head of black garlic, mix to a smooth paste with a few tablespoons of olive oil, then turn the chicken fillets in it. Cook for a few minutes in a shallow nonstick frying pan. When the chicken is almost ready, toss in a handful of whole, salted Marcona almonds.

Sort-of satay

Make a loose paste with crunchy peanut butter, white wine vinegar, crushed red pepper flakes, and a little whole-grain mustard. Spread onto the chicken fillets and cook in a shallow nonstick pan in a little olive oil.

Paprika, Mustard Chicken Goujons

chicken breast fillets, smoked paprika,
Dijon mustard, bread crumbs

Mix **3 heaping tablespoons of Dijon mustard** with **2 teaspoons of hot
smoked paprika** and a little salt and pepper. Season **14 ounces (400g)
boneless, skinless chicken breast fillets.** Put ½ **cup (25g) panko or
other crisp white bread crumbs** on a plate. Press the fillets first into
the mustard and paprika, then into the crumbs. Shallow-fry in
sunflower oil till crisp, then drain briefly on paper towels. Serve with
mayonnaise and wedges of lime.

For 2. Smoky, crunchy chicken.

Harissa Carrots

spring carrots, harissa paste, garlic, egg,
white wine vinegar, Dijon mustard

Trim the leaves of **1½ pounds (650g) spring carrots**, then blanch,
whole, in a deep pan of boiling, lightly salted water till tender. Peel
and mash **2 cloves of garlic** with a pestle and mortar or in a blender,
then blend with **an egg yolk, 4 tablespoons of olive oil, 1 tablespoon
of white wine vinegar, 1 tablespoon of Dijon mustard**, and **1 to
2 tablespoons of harissa paste**.

Drain the carrots carefully and place on a serving dish. Pour over
the dressing while the carrots are still warm and serve with steamed
brown rice.

For 4. The sweetness of carrots. The balance of spice.

One-Pan Sunday Lunch

chicken thighs, potatoes, white bread crumbs,
heavy cream, milk, butter, thyme, sage,
vegetable or chicken stock

You will need a large, shallow pan for this. Heat **a little oil** in the pan
and brown **4 chicken thighs** in it over moderate to high heat, then
remove them and set aside. Cut **14 ounces (400g) potatoes** into large
chunks and brown them in the chicken pan, adding more oil if
necessary. Return the chicken to the pan and pour in **1²/₃ cups (400ml)
hot vegetable or chicken stock**. Lower the heat, cover the pan with a
lid, and leave to cook for about 20 minutes.

Remove the chicken and potatoes from the pan. Pour **1¼ cups
(300ml) milk** and **½ cup (100ml) heavy cream** into the pan, scraping
at the toasty, crusty chicken bits on the base with a wooden spoon.
They will flavor the sauce. Add **3¹/₃ cups (150g) soft white bread
crumbs**, add **2 tablespoons of lemon thyme** (or just regular thyme),
and **a tablespoon of chopped sage leaves.** Season with salt and
pepper, then add **3 tablespoons (40g) butter** and whisk until you
have a smooth, creamy bread sauce. Pop the chicken and potatoes
back in to warm through, then serve.

For 2. Sunday lunch in a pan, for bread-sauce lovers.

A few variations on the turnips

Eggplant, orzo, and basil

Trim and finely dice a large eggplant, then fry in olive oil till soft and pale gold. Add a crushed clove of garlic, fry a minute or so longer, then season with shredded basil, a little lemon juice, and some salt. Cook 1 cup (150g) orzo as opposite, then stir it into the eggplant. Toss with a handful of grated Parmesan.

Roast pork, pasta

Add cooked, drained orzo to the roasting juices of a joint of roast pork. Stir gently and serve with the pork. The pasta will soak up the sticky juices from the pan.

A cure

Bring some homemade or good-quality purchased chicken stock to a boil. Add cooked, drained orzo, sea salt, and lemon juice, then finish with chopped mint. Cures most things for me.

Young Turnips with Mushrooms and Orzo

turnips, orzo pasta, mushrooms, shallot, arugula

Boil ⅔ **cup (100g) orzo pasta** in a large pot of salted water for about 9 minutes, till tender. Peel **a large shallot or small onion** and slice it finely, then fry in **a little butter or oil** till pale gold. Remove and set aside.

Slice **7 ounces (200g) young white turnips** into rounds about ⅛ inch (3mm) thick. Slice **3½ ounces (100g) button or small cremini mushrooms**. Fry both in **a little butter and oil** till golden brown. Return the fried shallot to the pan, then add **2 handfuls of arugula**.

Drain the cooked pasta and toss with the shallots, turnips, arugula, and mushrooms.

For 2. Earthy, frugal, and mild.

On the side of the cod

- A handful of mâche.
- Steamed green beans, tossed in chopped parsley.
- Mashed potato, a pool of it so buttery it almost slides from the plate.

And some variations

Hake, parsley, cream

Fry hake fillet in butter until pale gold underneath, then turn and cook the other side. Pour a small glass of white wine into the pan, add lots of chopped parsley, then heavy cream. Keep shaking the pan till you have a rough, impromptu sauce.

Pink fish, piquant sauce

Swap the cod opposite for salmon. Continue as in the recipe but, instead of tarragon and capers, add a tablespoon of brined green peppercorns and a little very finely chopped rosemary.

The scent of cardamom, the luxury of cream

Bring 1¼ cups (300ml) heavy cream to a boil, add about 10 lightly crushed cardamom pods, then remove from the heat and let it infuse. Fry fillets of snapper in a little butter in a nonstick frying pan, then pour in the cardamom-infused cream through a sieve to remove the pieces of crushed spice. Finish with salt, black pepper, and cilantro leaves. Eat with steamed rice.

Cod with Lemon, Tarragon, and Crème Fraîche

cod, lemons, tarragon, crème fraîche,
capers, bay leaf , butter, black peppercorns

Put **12 ounces (350g) cod fillet**, cut from the thick end of the fish, into a large, shallow pan with the **juice of 2 lemons** and **3 tablespoons (40g) butter**. Chop **half a small bunch of tarragon** and add to the pan with **a bay leaf** and **6 black peppercorns**. Bring to a boil, lower the heat, cover with a lid, and simmer for about 10 minutes, till the fish is opaque. Remove the fish with a spatula and keep warm.

Chop the rest of the bunch of tarragon and add it to the pan with **a teaspoon of capers** and **3 tablespoons of crème fraîche.** The crème fraîche will turn a little grainy where it meets the lemon juice. No matter. Spoon the sauce over the fish.

For 2. Soft, white, supremely citrus fish.

Eggplant and Chickpeas

eggplant, chickpeas, rosemary, garlic

Slice **a large eggplant** into thick rounds and place them in a single layer in a grill pan. Brush with **olive oil**, scatter with **a tablespoon of chopped rosemary needles**, salt, black pepper, and **2 cloves of finely crushed garlic**. Grill, adding **a little more oil** as necessary, for 10 minutes or so, until the eggplant is golden brown and thoroughly soft and tender. Turn each piece and allow to brown lightly on the other side.

Drain **a 14-ounce (400g) can of chickpeas** and warm half the contents in a small saucepan with **a little olive oil**, salt, and some black pepper. Process in a blender or food processor with half the grilled eggplant to give a soft, quite smooth puree. Fry the reserved chickpeas for a few minutes in **a little oil** in a shallow pan till hot, then stir, whole, into the eggplant and chickpea puree. Correct the seasoning, then serve with the warm, grilled eggplant and some torn sesame bread.

For 2. A textural thing.

A few thoughts on the spiced mushrooms

Commercial curry powders vary in heat and flavor, so use one whose qualities you know and trust, or of course mix your own.

If you want a creamy sauce, mix in a couple of tablespoons of yogurt just before you serve. Once any yogurt is added, remove from the heat or it will curdle.

Paneer or eggplant instead of mushrooms

Make a slower, more complex version by starting with chopped shallots and grated ginger and allowing them to soften before adding the mushrooms. Add more liquid, water or an extra can of tomatoes, and cook longer for a gentler, more mellow result. Introduce some herbs, such as cilantro and mint, at the end of the cooking time to brighten the flavor.

Spiced Mushrooms on Naan

mushrooms, curry powder, naan, canned tomatoes, green onions, chile, yogurt, mint

Warm **a few tablespoons of oil**, or **oil and a slice of butter**, in a deep pan over moderate heat, then add **3 chopped green onions** and **a finely sliced chile**. Cook until the onions are soft, then cut **7 ounces (200g) cremini mushrooms** into halves or quarters, depending on their size, and add them to the pan. As soon as the mushrooms start to lightly brown, stir in **a tablespoon of your favorite curry powder**, fry briefly, then add **a 14-ounce (400g) can of crushed tomatoes** and their juice. Season generously and leave to simmer for about 20 minutes, watching the pan carefully. Serve with warm **naan** and, if you wish, **a little yogurt** and **chopped mint**.

For 2. The nourishment of warm bread. The heat of spice.

Chile Shrimp with Watermelon

large shrimp, watermelon, red pepper flakes,
fish sauce, lime, sugar, flour, mint, cilantro

Mix **6½ tablespoons (50g) all-purpose flour** in a bowl with **a teaspoon of red pepper flakes** and a grinding of black pepper. Pour **4 tablespoons of Thai or Vietnamese fish sauce** into a bowl, stir in **a pinch of sugar—** no more—then add **14 ounces (400g) large, raw peeled shrimp** (fresh are best; defrosted are fine) and leave them for 15 minutes.

Heat **a thin film of oil** in a frying pan or wok, add the shrimp, and fry, moving them around as they cook, for a few minutes, until they are crisp and sweet. Remove from the pan and serve with the salad below.

Peel **a large wedge of watermelon** and pick out as many of the seeds as you can. Cut the flesh into large chunks and toss with **the juice of a lime, a few chopped mint leaves**, and **some torn cilantro**.

For 2. Mouth-popping shrimp. Refreshing watermelon.

A thought or two on risotto

Risotto is as much about texture as flavor. Ideally, it should be neither soupy nor stiff. It should slide slowly and gracefully from the wooden spoon rather than pour off it or have to be shaken. The creamy quality has as much to do with the rice as the stock—arborio rice and homemade chicken stock are preferred. But the desired texture can be aided by beating in a thick slice of butter with a wooden spoon at the end of the cooking time. The correct round-grain rice, good rich stock, and constant stirring will get you there.

For a change

Torn roast chicken, thyme, Parmesan

Sometimes, at the end of a long day, I am happy to stand at the stove and just stir.

Remove four double handfuls of meat from yesterday's roast chicken and tear it into small pieces. Make a classic risotto with 1 cup (200g) arborio rice and 4 cups (1 liter) or so of stock. As the risotto approaches its moment, stir in 2 teaspoons of chopped thyme leaves, the chicken, and a handful of grated Parmesan. Finish with a slice of butter and any jelly that may have set in the chicken's roasting pan.

Risotto

arborio rice, chicken stock, shallot, pancetta,
Parmesan

Peel **a shallot** and chop finely, then cut **5 ounces (150g) pancetta** into
small dice. Melt **a thick slice of butter** in a wide, shallow saucepan
and add the pancetta, then the onion. Leave to cook until the onion
is soft but not colored, stirring regularly so it doesn't brown. Add
1½ cups (300g) arborio rice, stirring to coat the grains in the butter
and pancetta fat, then add **2½ to 3 cups (600 to 700ml) hot chicken
stock**, a ladle at a time, stirring almost continuously. You will find the
rice will take about 20 minutes to cook. The consistency should be
thick and creamy.

   When the rice is ready, adjust the seasoning, adding a good **3 heaping
tablespoons of grated Parmesan** and a little black pepper and salt
(you may not need any salt at all), then spoon on to plates. For 4.

Roasted Vegetable Rice

red onion, eggplant, lemon, oregano,
garlic, mint, basmati rice

Finely slice **a medium-size red onion** and place in a roasting pan in
a single layer. Slice **an eggplant** into thick coins and add to the onion,
then squeeze over **the juice of a lemon** and tuck in **4 or 5 peeled garlic
cloves**. Dampen with about **4 tablespoons of olive oil**. Scatter with
dried oregano, then bake for 25 minutes at 350°F (180°C).

Cook **1 cup (200g) basmati rice** in **1²/₃ cups (400ml) water** until
tender. Add **3 tablespoons of mint**, and top with the roasted eggplant
and onion.

For 3. Homely. Aromatic. The joy of vegetables.

A variation on the penne with anchovies

Anchovies, olives, and basil croutons, a salad for high summer

Puree a couple of large handfuls of basil leaves with 4 tablespoons of olive oil, then warm in a frying pan. Add small chunks of torn-up ciabatta or baguette, letting them soak up the basil oil as they crisp. Toss them over a salad of marinated anchovies, black olives, red and yellow cherry tomatoes, mozzarella, and Little Gem lettuce with a glug or two of olive oil.

A can of anchovies, a few ideas

A can of anchovies in oil is an endlessly useful addition to the kitchen cupboard (I can eat them straight out of the can).
- Mash the drained anchovies into butter as a quick savory dressing for grilled lamb chops.
- Tuck into a soft, floury roll or piece of ciabatta with slices of tomato.
- Scrape out the insides of a baked potato, chop the drained anchovies, and fold into the potato with a slice of butter and black pepper, then pile back into the potato skin and return briefly to the oven.
- Chop drained anchovies and mash them with butter and a little black pepper, then spread over a leg of lamb and roast as usual.

Anchovy, Penne, Crumbs

marinated anchovies, small penne, butter,
bread crumbs, chile, lemon, parsley

Cook **1¼ cups (150g) mini penne pasta** in boiling water, then drain.

In a large nonstick pan, cook **a couple of handfuls of dried bread crumbs** in **a little oil** till golden, then remove. Add **3½ tablespoons (50g) butter** and **a chopped red chile**, then, 30 seconds later, add **the juice of half a lemon, 3½ ounces (100g) oil-packed anchovy fillets, a large handful of coarsely chopped parsley**, and the browned bread crumbs and drained penne. Toss briefly.

For 2. Soft, piquant, crisp, and hot.

A few ideas for smoked salmon

A smoked salmon sandwich

Rye bread, the light sort, toasted and spread with mayonnaise then layered with thickly cut smoked salmon, shatteringly crisp bacon, and a little crisp lettuce. If you stir some chopped dill into the mayo, then all the better.

Smoked salmon scramble

Shred the salmon into thin strips, then fold it into freshly made scrambled eggs with a twist of black pepper. It's a classic.

More interesting, perhaps, is to add a few bottled green peppercorns to the eggs; include chopped chives or stir in a little finely chopped cherry tomato, so the result is more like a coarse *piperade*.

Smoked Salmon and Green Peppercorn Macaroni

smoked salmon, macaroni, green peppercorns in brine, butter

Cook **1¼ cups (150g) macaroni** in boiling salted water. Shred **3½ ounces (100g) smoked salmon** into thin strips. Melt **3½ tablespoons (50g) butter** in a small pan and add **2 teaspoons of rinsed, bottled green peppercorns**. Drain the pasta in a colander and return to the pan, add the warm green peppercorn butter, and, just before eating, the strips of smoked salmon.

For 2. A light lunch. Gentle, delicate, and a little piquant.

Kipper Benedict

kipper fillets, egg yolks, butter, spinach,
English muffins, lemon

Put **1 pound (500g) kipper fillets** into a heatproof container or pan
and pour boiling water over them. Leave for 10 minutes, till the fish
will come off the bones fairly easily. Carefully remove every small bone.

Make a hollandaise. Soften **7 tablespoons (100g) butter** in a small
saucepan. Put **2 egg yolks** in a heatproof bowl over a pan of simmering
water. Slowly beat in the butter with a whisk, trickling it slowly into
the egg yolks. Season with **lemon juice** and salt, then remove from
the heat. Whisk it regularly to keep it from separating. Briefly steam
a handful of spinach leaves.

Split and toast **4 English muffins** and spoon a little hollandaise
onto each. Divide the spinach and kipper pieces among the muffins,
spoon over more hollandaise, and broil for a minute or two, till
golden, then eat immediately.

For 2. The reworking of an old breakfast favorite.

Little stews

Stew. Slow cooking. The bringing together of compatible flavors in liquid of some sort. Rich broth. Meat edging toward tenderness hour by hour. Comforting. Healing. Safe. Yes, all that and more. But we can have a stew on a weekday when time is against us, though we might have to rethink the word a little.

I make a great little stew, a fricassee, I suppose, with rabbit and tarragon, another with onions cooked till soft with black beans, and yet another with eggplant. They have all the qualities of slow-cooked food, yet mostly are made in less than an hour. In all fairness, not many use the bone-heavy, cheap cuts this method of cooking was designed for, but the essence of the stew is still there. The deep flavors, the aromatic liquid, the tender meat and vegetables. What isn't there is the hours of waiting.

Of course, nothing will quite beat the time-honored Irish stew, left to sort itself out in a low oven for a couple of hours. But that doesn't mean we can't have a lamb shank pot-roasted with plenty of liquid and root vegetables on the table in about an hour. We can also have chicken cooked on the bone with melting vegetables, a rich broth, and crisp skin.

There is much comfort in food that has been cooked in a Dutch oven. For the most part, it is winter cooking, the food that warms our soul. Initially saddened that it could never be part of a book about fast food, I took a long, hard look at how such recipes could be worked in order to fit in with the premise of having something good on the table within an hour or so of coming home on a working day. So here they are: a lamb dish with asparagus; a creamy, piquant chicken fricassee; a casserole of red cabbage and blue cheese; and a silky vegetable stew. Quick, warming dinners for cool days.

A few favorites

Lamb, garlic, paprika, and tomato
Crush 2 large, juicy cloves of garlic and mash them with 2 tablespoons of olive oil and a good pinch of salt. Add 1 pound (450g) cubed lamb, rolling it around until the meat is well seasoned with the paste. Peel and coarsely chop a medium onion and let it soften and lightly brown in a little oil over moderate heat. Add the meat to the pan, letting it brown here and there, tossing occasionally. Add two 14-ounce (400g) cans of chopped tomatoes and half a teaspoon of smoked paprika to the pan. Leave to simmer for 25 minutes over low heat. Just before eating, stir in about 4 ounces (120g) young spinach leaves and a handful of chopped cilantro and check the seasoning. Let the leaves wilt briefly, then eat. Thick chunks of bread are probably the most appropriate accompaniment.

Chicken, cream, a spike of tarragon vinegar
Slice 4 chicken breasts into thick strips, toss them in sizzling butter, and, when golden, add the leaves from 8 sprigs of tarragon, then, a minute later, 1 cup (250ml) heavy cream. Bring it to life with 2 to 3 teaspoons of tarragon vinegar.

Chicken thighs, golden skin, herbs, a flash of lemon
Let 4 chicken thighs, skin on and nicely seasoned, cook in a generous slice of butter in a shallow pan till their skin is crisp and golden. Pour in a glass of white wine, a medium-dry Riesling perhaps, then scrape at the crusted sediment with a wooden spoon, stirring it into the bubbling wine. Finish with chopped herbs: parsley, chervil, tarragon, dill—one or two only. Stir in the juice of a lemon and a last slice of butter, whisking it into the juices.

One thought on the slow-cooked rabbit

Not exactly a meal in minutes, this is nevertheless one of the simplest dinners possible. The preparation time is minimal.

And a few ideas for rabbit

Rabbit, asparagus, noodles, tarragon, and cream. A peaceful dinner

Cut 14 ounces (400g) boned rabbit meat into small pieces. Heat 3 tablespoons (40g) butter in a shallow pan, add the rabbit, and cook over moderate heat till delicately browned in patches. Add a bunch of asparagus, cut into short lengths, and a small bunch of chopped tarragon. Pour in a glass of dry vermouth or white wine and continue cooking for a few minutes, till the asparagus is tender. Boil about 8 ounces (250g) wide ribbon pasta in salted water and drain. Add a little cream or crème fraîche to the rabbit, check the seasoning, then drop in the drained pasta and toss gently. For 2 to 3.

Poached rabbit with carrots and orzo. A bowl of calm

For a pure, almost humble, meal, I like to poach a couple of rabbit pieces—the meaty leg or saddle—in vegetable stock with a few new season's carrots, sliced lengthwise, the most diminutive new potatoes I can find, a sprig of rosemary, and a couple of thyme sprigs, bay leaves, and black pepper. I let it simmer for as long as I have (30 to 40 minutes is about the minimum), then I scatter a couple of spoonfuls of orzo pasta into the broth. Ten minutes later you have a blissfully calming, almost soporific dish. Check the seasoning— it usually needs quite a bit of salt—and serve in a shallow bowl.

Slow-Cooked Rabbit with Herbs

rabbit, rosemary, thyme, tarragon, onions, wheat beer, heavy cream

You will need **1 pound (500g) rabbit, cut up by the butcher**. Peel and coarsely chop **2 onions**, then cook them in **a thick slice of butter** over moderate heat till they are translucent and pale gold. Season the pieces of rabbit all over with salt and black pepper. Push the onions to one side of the pan if there is room, or transfer them to a bowl if not, then add the rabbit pieces to the pan. Cook for 5 minutes, till appetizingly browned, turning as necessary, then mix the onions in.

Finely chop the needles from **2 small sprigs of rosemary** and add to the pan with **4 thyme sprigs, 4 cups (1 liter) of wheat beer**, and some salt and pepper. Bring to a boil, then lower the heat so the liquid continues cooking at a low simmer. Partially cover with a lid and leave to putter away on the stove for a couple of hours, till the rabbit is tender. The exact timing will depend on the age and provenance of your rabbit, but it is ready when you can remove the flesh from the bones with a decent table knife.

continued

The liquid in the pan will still be quite thin and plentiful, so turn up the heat for a few minutes until it has reduced by about half (this is not a thick sauce, and will always be the sort to eat with a spoon).

Pour in ½ **cup (100ml) heavy cream** and stir in the leaves from **4 lush sprigs of tarragon**, chopped if they are very long. Continue simmering for 5 to 10 minutes, then check the seasoning. For 2.

A thought on the lamb

This recipe can be padded out a bit if you want a more economical version. My feeling is for mushrooms. Cook them separately, in butter. When they are sticky on the outside, transfer them to the lamb, together with their buttery, fungal juices.

And a variation

Lamb, rosemary, and crème fraîche

Season 1 pound (450g) cubed lamb, brown it in a little oil, and remove from the pan. Lightly fry some coarsely chopped unsmoked bacon. Add a crushed clove of garlic, a little chopped rosemary, then some vegetable stock. Return the lamb to the pan, partially cover, and leave to simmer till the meat is tender. Stir in enough crème fraîche or sour cream to give thin but richly flavored juices.

Lamb with Asparagus

cubed lamb, asparagus, small onions,
white wine, stock, crème fraîche, chervil

Melt **3 tablespoons (40g) butter** in a deep Dutch oven, add **1 pound (450g) cubed lamb** (a tender cut, such as leg or fillet), and leave it to color lightly for a few minutes over moderate to high heat. Tossing it from time to time will help it color evenly on all sides. Remove the meat from the pan and set aside on a plate.

Peel **8 ounces (250g) small onions or large shallots**, keeping them whole but halving any that are bigger than an unshelled walnut. Add them to the pan and let them brown lightly, tossing them occasionally so they color fairly evenly.

Return the lamb and any of its juices that have escaped to the pan. Dust **2 tablespoons of all-purpose flour** over the meat and onions and cook for a minute or two, stirring from time to time. Turn up the heat and pour in **⅔ cup (150ml) white wine**. Leave the wine to bubble away till reduced by half, scraping at the crusty bits on the bottom of the pan with a wooden spatula as you go. Pour in **3⅓ cups (800ml) hot stock** (can be vegetable, lamb, or even chicken) and bring to a boil, then lower the heat and leave to simmer, partly covered, for about 30 minutes, until the meat is tender but still has plenty of bite.

continued

Lamb with Asparagus, *continued*

Slice **10 ounces (300g) asparagus spears** into 2 or 3 short lengths and add to the pan with salt and pepper. Continue cooking for about 5 minutes, till the asparagus is tender. Stir in **¾ cup (200ml) crème fraîche** and **a handful of chervil leaves.** Check the seasoning and serve.

For 4. Calm cooking for a spring day.

For a change from the chicken with sour cream

Roast chicken, herb mayo

Roast 4 chicken thighs with olive oil, lemon, thyme, and a few whole cloves of garlic in an oven set to 400°F (200°C). Let the skin darken and caramelize nicely. Make a herb mayonnaise, either from scratch (2 egg yolks, a squeeze of lemon, ⅔ cup / 150ml oil, ½ cup / 100ml olive oil) or using a good store-bought mayo. Stir in a small handful of chopped tarragon, a few chopped basil leaves, and just a couple of chopped chives. Remove the chicken meat from the bones, tear into jagged pieces, then tuck them among watercress and small, crisp lettuce heart leaves. Eat with French bread and the herb mayonnaise. (The garlic can be squeezed from its skin and stirred into the herb mayo, if you wish.)

Chicken and potato salad

Boil or steam 1 pound (500g) new potatoes, in their skins or peeled as you wish. Mix together 4 tablespoons of crème fraîche, a tablespoon of lemon juice, and 2 teaspoons of Dijon mustard. Remove the meat from the bones of the 4 roasted chicken thighs above, then toss gently with the crème fraîche dressing. Drain the potatoes and cut them in half, then toss them with the chicken and dressing. Eat as it is, or stuffed into a baguette.

Chicken with Sour Cream and Gherkins

chicken legs, sour cream, gherkins, Riesling, button mushrooms, shallots

Put **12 small shallots** in a bowl and pour boiling water over them. Set aside for 10 minutes to soften the skins and make them easier to peel. Season **2 large, free-range chicken legs**, then brown them lightly on either side in **a little butter** over moderate heat. Peel the shallots, add them to the pan, and let them color nicely all over.

Halve **8 ounces (250g) button mushrooms** and add them to the chicken and shallots, letting them color lightly. Thickly slice **6 gherkins**, then add to the pan together with **2 cups (500ml) Riesling**. Let the wine come to a boil, continue cooking at an enthusiastic bubble for 3 or 4 minutes, then lower the heat to a gentle simmer.

Cook for about 20 minutes, then stir in ⅔ **cup (150ml) sour cream**, keeping the heat quite low. Allow to warm through. Check the seasoning and serve with potatoes, noodles, or rice.

For 2. Smooth and a little piquant.

A few thoughts on the curry

You can mix your own masala, toasting and grinding spices to suit your taste, or you can use any of the ready-made spice mixes and curry powders available. When I am in the mood, I will toast cumin and coriander seeds, adding dried chile and turmeric. I will use cayenne and black pepper or occasionally a little ground clove. Often, I will finish a dish with garam masala. But, when I'm quickly putting together a curry, I use my favorite store-bought curry powder.

And a couple of variations

The earthy quality of chickpeas

Chickpeas can be used to make a curry go further. A couple of cans, drained and rinsed, can be added to the recipe opposite. Stir them in after the tomatoes. Alternatively, cook and serve the chickpeas separately: pour a little oil into a shallow pan, toast a teaspoon of cumin seeds in it, then add a peeled and finely chopped onion. Cook until soft, then add a little grated ginger, a teaspoon of ground coriander, and a pinch of turmeric. Stir in a can of drained chickpeas. Finish with a little garam masala, salt, and a squeeze of lemon juice.

Eggplant, with the brightness of tomatoes

Warm 2 tablespoons of oil in a saucepan, add a chopped onion, cook until softened, then stir in half a teaspoon of turmeric and half a teaspoon of garam masala, a little ground chile, and a couple of crushed garlic cloves. Add 4 tomatoes, coarsely chopped, and 2 red chiles, then enough water to make a loose sauce. In a separate pan, cook the eggplant as opposite, letting it color lightly in the oil. Stir the eggplant into the tomatoes, then continue cooking for 20 minutes. Turn the heat up to boil off any excess liquid and stir in a handful of cilantro leaves. Eat with rice.

Eggplant Curry

eggplants, onions, tomatoes, garlic, curry powder, garam masala, ginger, cilantro, yogurt

Peel **2 medium onions** and coarsely chop them. Thickly slice **2 medium eggplants**. Cook the onions and eggplant in **6 tablespoons of oil** in a large, deep pan. As they soften, peel and thinly slice **2 cloves of garlic** and add to the pan with **a tablespoon of finely chopped fresh ginger**. Stir in **2 tablespoons of mild curry powder** and fry briefly. Chop **1½ pounds (700g) tomatoes**, add to the pan, and leave to simmer for 25 minutes, till the curry has thickened.

Season with salt, pepper, and **a tablespoon of garam masala**. Finish with **a little fresh cilantro** and offer **yogurt** at the table. Eat with steamed rice or warm flatbread.

For 4 to 6. Satisfying, curiously refreshing.

Black Bean and Onion Stew

black beans, pancetta, onion, rosemary,
vegetable stock, basil

Coarsely chop **a large onion**. Melt **a thick slice of butter** in a deep pan
and cook the onion in it till soft and pale gold. Cut **a thick slice of
pancetta (about 3½ ounces / 100g)** into cubes and add to the onion,
cooking the pancetta till the fat becomes translucent.

Add **a 14-ounce (400g) can of black beans or black-eyed peas,
a bushy rosemary sprig**, and **3⅓ cups (800ml) vegetable stock**, then
simmer for 15 to 20 minutes. Season generously, add **a handful of
whole basil leaves**, then serve.

For 4. Sweet. Silky. Restoring.

Another idea

Squash with chile and orange

Peel 2 pounds (1kg) winter squash, cut into large cubes, and steam for
15 minutes till tender to the point of a knife. Finely chop a medium-
hot red chile without removing the seeds. In a bowl, mix the chopped
chile, the finely grated zest of an orange, a little salt and black pepper,
and 5 tablespoons of panko. Toss the squash in the crumbs, then fry
in a shallow layer of oil in a nonstick pan. When the crumbs are
golden, lift out and serve. If you have a little tomato sauce knocking
around, then all the better. For 4.

For when the tomatoes are at their best

Tomatoes, artichokes, basil croutons

Preheat the oven to 350°F (180°C). Pour 7 tablespoons of olive oil into
a blender. Tear up scant 1 cup (20g) basil and add it to the oil, then
process to a smooth green puree. Cut 3½ ounces (100g) good crusty
bread into large cubes, put in a baking dish, then pour over the basil
oil. Toss the bread till it is coated in the basil oil, then bake for
15 minutes till lightly crisp on the outside but still soft in the center.

Halve 14 ounces (400g) juicy, perfectly ripe tomatoes of various
colors and toss with 5 ounces (150g) sliced, marinated artichokes (the
sort they have at the deli counter or in jars at the supermarket). Tuck
them in among the hot croutons and eat while the croutons are still
warm. For 2.

Belgian Endive with Grapes, Honey, and Mustard

Belgian endive, grapes, honey, whole-grain mustard

Trim **3 heads of Belgian endive** and cut them in half from tip to root. Halve **7 ounces (200g) grapes** and seed them. Melt **3 tablespoons (40g) butter** in a wide, shallow pan for which you have a lid, add the endive, cut side down, and cook over moderate heat for 3 or 4 minutes, covered with the lid, till the underside is taking on a little color and there is a little translucency to the leaves, then turn. Add the grapes to the pan, continue cooking briefly till they soften, then remove the endive and grapes to a serving dish. Stir **1 tablespoon of whole-grain mustard** and **2 tablespoons of honey** into the butter, heat for a minute or so, then pour over the endive and grapes.

For 2. Soft, slightly bitter leaves, sweet honey. Light lunch. A side for air-dried ham.

A few thoughts on the lamb shanks

- Lamb shanks take a long time to cook, but they need minimal preparation (which is why they have found a place in this book). Just a bit of chopping and stirring, then the oven does most of the work. Choose small shanks so that they will cook in an hour and a half. Save larger ones from older animals for the weekend. It is not strictly necessary to brown the shanks before adding the stock, but if you do there will be even more flavor in the juices.
- Use large winter carrots so they don't collapse into the cooking liquid.
- Keep the mash rough and ready.

And a couple of variations

A Provençal version

Use a light and fruity red wine instead of stock. Try adding rosemary sprigs or a strip of orange peel to the pan. Remove the root vegetables with a slotted spoon and beat to a smooth and silky puree with some of the cooking liquid.

The richness of port

Use half port, half stock. Add soft prunes and a few raisins. Serve with red cabbage that you have cooked in a lidded pot with coriander seeds, red wine vinegar, a finely chopped red chile, and a little vegetable stock.

Lamb Shanks with Crushed Roots

lamb shanks, carrots, parsnips, stock, thyme

Peel **1 pound (500g) each of large carrots** and **parsnips** and cut into rough chunks, then brown them lightly all over in **a little olive oil** over moderate heat in an ovenproof dish. Place **2 small lamb shanks** on top of the vegetables, pour over **2 cups (500ml) stock** (lamb, chicken, or vegetable), tuck in **a bunch of thyme**, season with salt and pepper, then cover the dish tightly with a lid. Bake in an oven set at 350°F (180°C) for 1½ hours, then remove the shanks, thyme, and most of the liquid to a warm place.

Using the small amount of liquid in the dish, coarsely crush the roots with a potato masher or fork and serve with the shanks and the reserved juices.

For 2, generously. A hearty, untroublesome roast.

A few ideas for chicken

Chicken breasts, garlic, thyme, a sweet glaze of muscat wine

Finely dice a little onion, carrot, and celery, then toss them in a bowl with 4 crushed cloves of garlic, the leaves from 3 or 4 bushy sprigs of thyme, and a couple of glasses of sweet muscat wine. Add 4 chicken breasts or thighs and leave to marinate for a good hour or more. Place the chicken under a hot broiler, 4 to 5 inches (10 to 13cm) from the heat, spooning over the marinade as it cooks. It is ready when the juices run clear when the meat is pierced with a skewer.

Crisp golden chicken skin, soft green leaves, salt flakes

Remove the skin from 2 chicken legs or 4 thighs or drumsticks. Lay the skin on a baking sheet, season lightly, then bake or broil till crisp and deep gold. Drain on paper towels and break it into small pieces. Dress 2 handfuls of soft butter lettuce with olive oil, Dijon mustard, and lemon. Generously season the crisp chicken skin with sea salt flakes, then tuck it among the soft leaves. French bread. Cold butter.

Cider Thighs

chicken thighs, dry cider, cremini
mushrooms, onions, potatoes, rosemary,
black peppercorns, bay leaves

Remove and reserve the skin from **6 large chicken thighs**, then fry
the thighs in **a little oil** in a large, shallow pan. Halve **3½ ounces
(100g) cremini mushrooms**. Peel and coarsely chop **2 medium onions**
and add them to the pan together with the mushrooms. Cut
2 baking-size potatoes into 4 pieces each and tuck them into the pan.

Add **the leaves from 2 sprigs of rosemary, 6 whole black peppercorns**,
and **a couple of bay leaves** and then pour in **3 cups (750ml) dry hard
cider**. Bring to a boil, lower the heat, and simmer for 40 minutes.

Salt and generously pepper the reserved chicken skin, then put it
under a hot broiler until crisp. Using a fork, crush half the potato pieces
into the sauce, leaving the others whole. Serve the meat, sauce, and
potatoes in a shallow bowl topped with the crisped chicken skin, with a
spoon for the sauce. Lightly cooked shredded green cabbage on the side.

For 3. Crisp skin, crisp cider, plump chicken.

Some ideas for blue cheese

Blue cheese rabbit

Split and lightly toast an English muffin. Mash together some soft blue cheese (Cashel blue, Gorgonzola, Picos, Roquefort, whatever) and a few spoonfuls of butter. Spread generously onto the toasted muffin halves and broil till sizzling lightly.

Blue cheese, new potatoes

Boil new potatoes, or at least small potatoes, in a large pot of lightly salted water, then drain. While they are still hot, slice them in half and place in a heatproof dish. Generously crumble over blue cheese such as Stichelton or Stilton, then place under a hot broiler or in the oven till the cheese has melted.

Blue cheese, figs, and a baguette

Ripe figs, soft blue cheese. You have a magical marriage of flavors and textures there. Even more so if you add some coarsely torn shards of slightly burned, shatteringly crisp baguette.

Stewed Red Cabbage with Blue Cheese and Apple

red cabbage, blue cheese, pippin apples,
white wine vinegar, sourdough bread

Finely shred **8 ounces (250g) red cabbage**. Cut **2 pippin apples, or apples of another crisp variety**, into segments. Warm **2 tablespoons of peanut oil** in a deep pan, add the cabbage and apples, and cook, stirring from time to time, till the cabbage starts to wilt and the apples have softened a little. Pour in ½ **cup (100ml) white wine vinegar** and let it sizzle.

Tear **a thick slice of sourdough bread** into rough croutons and fry in **a little oil or butter** till golden and crisp. Drain briefly on paper towels.

Divide the cabbage and apple between 2 plates. Dice **6 ounces (175g) blue cheese** and add it to the plates together with the sourdough croutons.

For 2. Piquant, crisp. The rich luxury of blue cheese.

Chicken with Fennel
and Leek

chicken thighs, fennel, leeks, stock,
lemon, parsley

Season **6 bone-in chicken thighs** with salt and pepper, then brown
them lightly in a shallow pan in **a little oil** and **melted butter**. Cut
2 medium-size leeks into cork-size lengths, wash thoroughly, then
add to the pan. Separate **2 fennel bulbs** into layers, then add them
to the chicken and leeks and leave to soften for about 10 minutes,
covering with a lid. Grate in the **zest from a lemon** and continue
cooking for a minute or so.

Scatter **2 tablespoons of flour on top**, then cook for a few minutes
before pouring in **4 cups (1 liter) of chicken or vegetable stock**. Bring
to a boil, season, then lower the heat to a simmer and leave to cook
for 35 minutes, covered with a lid, giving the occasional stir.

Finish the dish with **the juice of the lemon** and **a handful of
chopped parsley**. We have leeks and fennel already, so just starchy
potatoes, steamed in their skins, to soak up the parsley-freckled
chicken juices.

For 3. Familiar flavors. A meal to nourish.

In the oven

Food cooked in the oven gets on with the job itself, without us having to watch over it. No tinkering, stirring, or moving it around the pan. No having to lower the heat or prod and poke. We simply put a dish in the oven and leave it to do its stuff. That is not to say a roast won't benefit from the occasional basting with its juices, or that you can ignore a rapidly browning pie, but it does allow us time to do other things while our dinner cooks.

Many of the dishes in this section take a good half hour, even an hour or longer, in the oven. They belong in this book because their preparation time is minimal and, once they are in the oven, we are free to do something else. I like the idea of fifteen minutes of hands-on cooking followed by an hour in the oven. Anything that takes a long time both to prepare and cook is excluded.

A roasting pan is an essential piece of equipment for anyone with an eye on a traditional Sunday lunch, but other baking dishes are important too. A shallow dish of enamel, ovenproof china, or even glass is good for a layered dish of pasta or a pie, but it can also be used to bake stuffed vegetables and sausages. My enamel dishes are secondhand and much loved. Pottery baking dishes can become beautifully worn with time and even heatproof glass, possibly the least romantic of all cookware, has a pleasing homeliness to it. You don't need many, maybe just a nest of enamel dishes of different sizes.

The most straightforward of oven dishes, the roast chicken, has its cooking time shortened here by being cut into pieces—legs and thighs mostly—and, in one case, the bird is butterflied. While a whole roast chicken, with butter and thyme or lemon, could possibly fit into a book of fast food, it is probably more useful to include recipes for roast chicken pieces that take half the time of a whole bird. Here you will find baked chicken with Taleggio, a stuffed breast with smoked cheese, and spicy marmalade drumsticks. There is a quick stuffed squid whose filling of beans makes you think you are eating a dish that has been cooking for hours in a slow oven.

The essence of baking or roasting is not only its simplicity and good-natured quality but also what happens to the food. Juices leak and caramelize on the pan, edges crisp, flavors concentrate. Even roasted for a short time, chicken pieces will develop a crisp, savory skin; the filling for a stuffed chicken breast will melt appetizingly; a belly of lamb will tenderize. But there is more. Pasta in a sauce will form a golden crust, vegetables baked in cheese sauce will turn an irresistible gold, a potato will bake to bring untold comfort.

The oven is particularly good for fish, such as sea bass and red mullet with leeks. Here, the time-heavy layered dishes such as lasagne have been shortened by replacing the ragù sauce with layers of herby sausage meat. There is also a series of little roasts, including boneless lamb loin chops with seasoned crumbs and satay drumsticks with bean sprouts and curry paste. Food that needs little interference from us once the initial preparation is over. Dinner that almost cooks itself.

A few favorite oven dinners

Lime and honey
Put chicken thighs in a roasting pan, mix runny honey and lime juice to taste, season with salt and pepper, then pour over the chicken. Turn skin side up, then roast in an oven set at 400°F (200°C) till the skin is golden and the juices run clear. Salt generously as you eat.

Pork with apples and maple syrup
Coarsely chop a couple of apples, discarding the cores. Peel and coarsely chop an onion. Mix the two, then roast in a little oil in an oven set at 400°F (200°C) for 15 minutes. Season a pork tenderloin with salt, pepper, and fennel seeds, then sear in a pan with hot oil. Add the pork to the roasting pan, drizzle maple syrup on top, and roast for about 30 minutes, depending on the weight, then leave to rest.

Soy chicken. Oh so sticky
Mix ⅔ cup (150ml) oyster sauce, 2 tablespoons of soy sauce, 2 tablespoons of light muscovado sugar, half a teaspoon of red pepper flakes, 2 chopped green onions, and 2 chopped garlic cloves. Put 4 chicken pieces into a baking dish, pour in the sauce, and toss gently to coat. Bake at 400°F (200°C) for 20 minutes, baste with the sauce, then cook for another 15 to 20 minutes, keeping an eye on it—it burns easily. Serve with bean sprouts, crisp lettuce, or watercress. For 2.

Potatoes with Spices
and Spinach

potatoes, cayenne, red pepper flakes, turmeric,
cumin, garlic, spinach, shallots, yogurt, cilantro

Cut **1¾ pounds (800g) large starchy potatoes** into big pieces and cook
in a large pot of salted water for about 15 minutes, till approaching
tenderness. Peel **5 large shallots** and halve them lengthwise. Drain the
potatoes, then put them in a bowl, add the shallots, and toss with **half
a teaspoon of cayenne, a teaspoon of red pepper flakes, a teaspoon of
crushed garlic,** and **a teaspoon each of ground cumin** and **turmeric.**
Add **2 teaspoons of sea salt flakes** and **4 tablespoons of peanut oil,**
then transfer to a roasting pan and bake at 400°F (200°C) until crisp.
Wash **a couple of large handfuls of spinach.** Put them in a pan over
moderate heat, cover with a lid, and leave for a minute or two to wilt.
Toss with the crisp potatoes, a **little yogurt,** and **torn cilantro.**
　　Enough for 2 to 3. Hot, cool, crisp, soft.

Some variations on the bacon boulangère

Rust-red chorizo, green leaves

In the recipe opposite, substitute about 14 ounces (400g) chorizo for the bacon. Flat-leaf parsley, coarsely chopped, is pleasing to find in the stock.

Earthy, beefy porcini, the zing of lemon

Pour boiling water over about ½ cup (10g) dried porcini and let them soak for 10 minutes. When they are soft, layer them with the potatoes. Add the juice of half a lemon and a handful of parsley to the stock. You could use the porcini soaking water for some of the stock to bring a deep miso-like quality to the dish.

Golden rutabaga, green dill, and a little fish

Peel and slice a rutabaga. Soften very thinly sliced onions in a little butter or oil. Layer alternately, adding chopped anchovies and finely chopped dill.

Celery root and duck confit

Peel and thinly slice a celery root. Rub a baking dish with duck fat, then layer the celery root with duck confit (from a can or jar) pulled off the bone and a little chopped thyme. I like to brown the confit a little in a nonstick frying pan first, then layer it with the sliced celery root. Bake as opposite. Celery root can also be used in the bacon version opposite.

Bacon Boulangère

potatoes, bacon, vegetable stock

Scrub **12 ounces (350g) large starchy potatoes** then slice them about ⅛ inch (3mm) thick. Cut **10 slices of bacon** lengthwise into three pieces each.

   In an ovenproof dish, layer the potatoes and bacon, seasoning with salt and pepper as you go. Pour in **2 cups (500ml) vegetable stock**, cover the dish with foil, and bake for an hour at 400°F (200°C). Remove the foil and continue to cook for 15 minutes, till brown.

   Serve with a crisp salad of iceberg-style lettuce and peppery watercress.

   For 4. Frugal, plain, and simple. Peaceful starch and soothing stock with a back note of smoke.

Summer Squash Gratin

Summer squash, mushrooms, basil,
mozzarella, béchamel sauce, Parmesan

Preheat the oven to 400°F (200°C). Peel **a large summer squash**; it should then weigh about 1½ pounds (750g). Halve lengthwise, remove and discard the seeds and any fibers, then slice ⅛ inch (3mm) thick. Warm **a little butter and oil** in a shallow pan. As it starts to bubble, lower in a few of the squash slices in a single layer and let them color a little underneath. Turn them over and cook the other side—they should be translucent and tender. Remove them and drain on paper towels. Continue with the rest of the squash slices.

While the squash is cooking, thickly slice **10 ounces (300g) mushrooms**. When all the squash is done, add the mushrooms to the pan, with **a little more butter** if necessary, season them with salt and pepper, then, as they are approaching doneness, stir in ⅔ **cup (15g) basil leaves**. Once they have wilted, remove the pan from the heat.

Cover the bottom of a large, shallow baking dish with some of the squash and mushroom mixture. Tear **a ball of mozzarella** into pieces and dot them over the mushroom mixture. Spoon **2 cups (500ml) béchamel sauce** (ready-made is fine) over the surface, then add another layer of squash, seasoning as you go. Finally, top with **a generous dusting of grated Parmesan**. Bake for about 40 minutes, till the sauce is bubbling, the top gently browned.

For 4 to 6. A delight for folks haunted by an extra-big summer squash in their vegetable box.

A few thoughts on the roast lamb

- Boneless lamb loin chops are lean; be generous with the olive oil.
- Use coarse, dry bread crumbs, ideally panko. Scatter any leftover crumbs in the dish and serve them on the side.

And for a change

Pistou

Spread pistou over the lamb instead of the mustard, and swap the cumin and caraway seeds for herbes de Provence (savory, basil, thyme, lavender). Roast as opposite. On the side: green beans.

Wasabi and panko

Spread the browned lamb with wasabi paste (freshly grated from the root if at all possible), then roll it in the bread crumbs. Roast as opposite.

Pistachio and black olive tapenade

Spread the warm, seared lamb chops with black olive tapenade, roll them in crushed pistachios, and roast as opposite.

Harissa and sesame

Spread a layer of harissa paste over the browned lamb, roll lightly in sesame seeds, then roast as opposite.

Mustard

Spread a pork tenderloin with Dijon mustard and wrap in bread crumbs the same way as the lamb opposite, but double the cooking time, basting halfway through. Eat with apple puree and a fennel and watercress salad.

Roast Lamb, Mustard, and Crumbs

lamb loin chops, bread crumbs, cumin seeds, caraway seeds, Dijon mustard

Trim **a couple of boneless lamb loin chops, each weighing about 10 ounces (300g)**. Mix **½ cup (50g) dried bread crumbs, a tablespoon of cumin seeds**, and **a tablespoon of caraway seeds** together and set aside. Warm **a film of oil** in a shallow nonstick pan, season the lamb with salt and pepper, then brown them briefly in the oil.

Remove the lamb chops from the pan and spread them with **Dijon mustard**. I do this quite generously, but it depends on your taste for the stuff. Then roll them in the seasoned crumbs. Drizzle with **a light coating of olive oil**, then bake for about 10 minutes in an oven preheated to 400°F (200°C). Remove from the oven and leave to rest for 5 to 10 minutes. Slice and serve. Depending on the time of year, green beans, spinach, potatoes au gratin, or new potatoes would be an appropriate accompaniment.

For 4. Rose meat. Golden crumbs.

For a change from the marmalade chicken

For a warmer (but far from hot) version, add a pinch of red pepper flakes to the marmalade mix, or a little finely chopped shallot or onion. Score the chicken all over with a knife, then massage and spread the marmalade down into the slashes.

Mustard, mango chutney, Worcestershire sauce, a spiced chicken sandwich

Mix together a tablespoon or so of Dijon mustard, 2 crushed cloves of garlic, a couple of tablespoons of mango chutney, and a tablespoon of Worcestershire sauce. Deeply slash a couple of cold cooked chicken legs, smooth the spice paste over them, then cook under the broiler till sizzling. Cut the meat from the bone, then stuff into soft, floury white buns.

A sweet, sticky coating

Make a mixture of runny honey, molasses, whole-grain mustard, and tomato ketchup. The result should be sweet, with a back note of heat from the mustard. Toss the drumsticks till well coated, then bake as opposite, keeping a close eye on them. If they appear to be browning too quickly, cover them with foil.

Marmalade Chicken

chicken drumsticks, marmalade,
whole-grain mustard

Put **6 large chicken drumsticks** on a foil-lined baking sheet or in a
small roasting pan. Mix **6 heaping tablespoons of marmalade** with
3 tablespoons of whole-grain mustard and a grinding of black
pepper. Spoon the seasoned marmalade over the chicken and bake
for about 30 minutes in an oven set at 400°F (200°C), keeping an
eye on them so they don't burn.

For 2 to 3. Sweet, spicy, succulent.

A few variations on the chicken and pancetta

Garlic, shallots, butter, and bread crumbs

In a food processor or by hand, mix 5 tablespoons (75g) butter, a handful of fresh, coarse bread crumbs, 2 finely chopped shallots, 2 cloves of garlic, and a small handful of chopped parsley. Partially cook a couple of oiled, boned chicken thighs or breasts under a broiler. As the meat approaches readiness, spread the bread crumb paste over it and continue broiling, basting occasionally, till golden.

Pancetta and mustard

Finely chop a few slices of pancetta or bacon in a food processor, then mix with soft, fresh bread crumbs, melted butter, and a little Dijon mustard to bind. Spread over the chicken breasts and cook under a moderately hot broiler.

Chicken Breast with Smoked Cheese and Pancetta

chicken breasts, pancetta, green onions, smoked cheese

Slice deeply into the long edge of **2 plump chicken breasts** to make a large pocket in each one. Chop **3½ ounces (100g) pancetta** into small dice. Fry till crisp in a shallow pan, add **2 chopped green onions**, and continue cooking till the fat is golden, then transfer to a bowl. Mix in **3½ ounces (100g) cubed smoked cheese**, then season with salt and black pepper.

Stuff the filling into the chicken breasts and seal with a wooden skewer or two. Bake in an oven set at 350°F (180°C) for 25 to 30 minutes, till golden. Remove the skewers and serve.

For 2. Golden chicken. Smoky, molten cheese.

A couple of dishes inspired by the baked mullet

Sea bass, waxy potatoes

Place a layer of sliced waxy potatoes in a roasting pan. Toss them with olive oil, shreds of bacon, and a little chopped rosemary. Place a cleaned whole sea bass on top, rub with oil and rosemary, and bake as opposite.

A whole baked fish with eggplant

Cut a couple of eggplants into small cubes of about ⅜ inch (1cm) or so. Toss them in plenty of olive oil, salt, and chopped thyme. Place in a roasting pan and bake for about 30 minutes at 350°F (180°C), tossing occasionally so they cook evenly. When they are golden and thoroughly soft, place a cleaned and prepared whole fish (red or gray mullet, red snapper, whole sardines) on top, then drizzle generously with olive oil, the juice of half a lemon, and plenty of salt and pepper. Bake till the flesh of the fish is firm. The exact time will depend on the weight and variety of your fish, but allow about 20 to 40 minutes. Serve with extra oil and lemon.

Baked Red Mullet with Fennel and Leeks

red mullet, fennel, leeks, parsley, lemon

Preheat the oven to 350°F (180°C). Halve and trim **5 ounces (150g) young fennel**. If you are using a plump, older bulb, then shred it finely. Trim **5 ounces (150g) young leeks**, leaving them whole if they are thin and small; if not, halve them lengthwise. Toss the vegetables with **4 tablespoons of olive oil**. Throw in **a little chopped parsley** and **the juice of a lemon**. Transfer the mixture to a roasting tin. Place **2 red mullet**, prepared and trimmed, on top of the vegetables. Brush them with oil from the pan, then bake for 20 minutes or so.

For 2. Bright leeks, sweet fish.

Tomatoes with an Anchovy Crumb Crust

tomatoes, anchovies, white bread, basil, cilantro,
parsley, green onions

Set the oven at 350°F (180°C). Put **4 tablespoons of olive oil** into a
deep frying pan set over moderate heat. Slice **6 green onions** and
add them to the pan. Halve **2 pounds (1kg) tomatoes** horizontally
and add them to the pan too. Cover with a lid and cook for 5 minutes
or so, till the tomatoes have softened but are still holding their
shape. Add **a chopped tomato** to the pan with **a handful of basil** and
cilantro leaves, a grinding of black pepper, and a very little salt, then
turn off the heat.

Blitz **2 ounces (60g) white bread** in a food processor till you have
soft, coarse crumbs, then add **a handful of parsley, 5 anchovies**, and
a little black pepper and process again briefly. Transfer the tomatoes
and their cooking juices to an ovenproof dish, scatter the crumb crust
over them, and bake for 30 minutes, until the tomatoes are sizzling
and the crust is deep gold.

For 4. Provence!

A thought on the butterflied chicken

Cutting through the chicken requires a good strong knife, but your butcher should be pleased to help if you prefer. The recipe can be used with chicken pieces too. Thighs and whole legs probably work best.

And a variation or two

Sesame and mirin

Rub chicken drumsticks with butter, salt, and pepper and roast them. When brown and almost ready, toss in a mixture of toasted sesame oil and mirin, scatter over a few sesame seeds, and continue roasting.

Orange and sherry vinegar

Stir a little sherry vinegar into orange juice, add a little melted butter, then pour over chicken thighs or a butterflied chicken. Tuck the empty orange shells underneath and roast as opposite.

Butterflied Chicken, Arugula, Couscous

chicken, arugula, couscous, lemon, young garlic, chicken stock, thyme

Preheat the oven to 400°F (200°C). Place **a medium-size chicken** on a chopping board and, using a heavy, sharp knife, cut through the backbone and open the chicken out flat. (If you don't want to do this yourself, you can ask the butcher to do it.) Place the chicken, skin side up, in a roasting pan. In a small bowl or jar, mix **4 tablespoons of olive oil** and the **juice of a lemon** (keep the empty shells). Season with salt and pepper, then add the leaves from **3 or 4 thyme sprigs**. Spoon or pour the oil mixture over the chicken, then add **a further 8 or so thyme sprigs**. Cut **a head of young garlic** in half and tuck the halves in around the meat, together with the empty lemon shells.

Roast the chicken for no longer than 45 minutes, by which time the skin should be golden brown and the juices should run clear when pierced with a skewer in the thickest part of the flesh.

continued

Remove the roasting pan from the oven and put the chicken on a warm plate, covered with foil, to rest. Add **2 cups (500ml) chicken stock** into the roasting pan and gently scrape at the roasting sediment left in the pan, letting it dissolve in the stock, then tip in **1⅓ cups (250g) couscous**, spread fairly evenly, cover the pan tightly with foil or a cloth, and leave to swell for 10 minutes.

Wash **3½ ounces (100g) arugula leaves**, then mix them into the couscous with a fork, loosening the grains as you fold the leaves in. Add a little salt and pepper as you think fit and **a little lemon juice** to taste. Cut the chicken into pieces and serve with the arugula couscous.

For 4. Couscous plumped up with the roasting juices and pan drippings. No flavors go to waste.

A few ideas inspired by the sea bass and beans

A late-night sardine supper

Drain a can of cannellini beans, put them into a pan, and add a little butter and olive oil. Warm them over moderate heat. Open a can of good-quality sardines in olive oil, break them up into large pieces, then fold them into the beans. Season with salt, pepper, and a little red wine vinegar. Hardly a gourmet feast, but worth a thought when you're hungry and perhaps a little the worse for wear.

The reassurance of a classic

Heat the contents of a can or jar of lentils in a generous amount of olive oil, adding a crushed clove of garlic, some salt and pepper, a few leaves of thyme, and maybe a bay leaf or two. Simmer gently, stirring regularly. In a shallow pan, fry half a dozen scallops, or a piece of cod, in foaming butter. Toss in a handful of chopped parsley, add a splash of red wine vinegar, and serve with the lentils.

Sea Bass with Tarragon Flageolets

sea bass, flageolet beans, tarragon,
soft butter, lemon

Mash ⅔ **cup (150g) soft butter** with **a good handful of chopped
tarragon leaves** and **a tablespoon of lemon juice**. Season with salt and
pepper and set aside.

Preheat the oven to 400°F (200°C). Season **a large sea bass or
2 smaller ones** inside and out. Tuck half the tarragon butter inside
the belly cavity, then lightly seal it closed by threading a wooden
skewer or cocktail stick through it. Place the fish in a roasting pan.

Drain and rinse **two 14-ounce (400g) cans of flageolet beans**. Surround
the fish with the flageolets and dot the remaining tarragon butter
over the beans. Wrap a piece of foil loosely over the top, then bake for
about 40 minutes, depending on the size of your fish. For the last
15 minutes of cooking, spoon or brush some of the buttery juices over
the fish and return it to the oven without the foil. Break the fish into
4 pieces to serve and spoon over the beans and juice.

For 4. Silky fish, soft beans.

Satay Drumsticks

chicken drumsticks, peanut butter, Thai red
curry paste, rice wine vinegar, toasted sesame
oil, tamarind paste, sugar, bean sprouts

Preheat the oven to 400°F (200°C). Put **1 cup (250g) crunchy peanut
butter** in a mixing bowl with **2 tablespoons of Thai red curry paste,
2 tablespoons of rice vinegar, 2 tablespoons of toasted sesame
oil, 2 tablespoons of tamarind paste, 3 tablespoons of golden baker's
sugar**, and **1²/₃ cups (400ml) water**. Stir well, then pour over **8 large
chicken drumsticks** and bake for about 45 minutes. Remove the
drumsticks to a warm plate, toss **1¹/₂ cups (150g) bean sprouts** through
the sauce left in the pan, and serve with the drumsticks.

For 4. Nutty. Spicy. Delicious fingers to lick.

Squid Stuffed with Judión Beans and Tomato

squid, judión or butter beans, tomatoes,
garlic, rosemary, dry sherry

Peel and finely slice **4 garlic cloves**, then fry in **a thin layer of olive oil** in a deep frying pan till very lightly colored. Cut **8 tomatoes** into roughly 8 pieces each, then add to the garlic together with the chopped leaves from **a bushy sprig of rosemary**. Cook for 6 or 7 minutes, till the mixture is soft, fragrant, and quite juicy. Season with salt and black pepper.

Drain 1½ **pounds (650g) judión beans or butter beans** of any liquid in the can or jar, rinsing them in a colander if you wish, then stir them gently into the tomato mixture and continue cooking over moderate heat for 5 minutes. Remove from the heat. Preheat the oven to 400°F (200°C).

Check **4 prepared medium squid**, making sure that they are thoroughly clean and the transparent quills have been removed from the body sacs and discarded. Set aside the tentacles. Using a tablespoon, stuff the squid bodies with as much of the filling as you can, laying them down slightly apart in a roasting pan or large baking dish. Spoon any excess filling into the roasting pan.

continued

Squid Stuffed with Judión Beans and Tomato, *continued*

Pour 1¼ cups (300ml) **dry sherry** around the squid, add **a couple more rosemary sprigs** to the pan, and bake for 20 to 25 minutes, occasionally basting the squid with the sherry. Halfway through cooking, tuck the reserved tentacles around the squid bodies.

Serve the squid and tentacles in shallow bowls or on deep plates, spooning the thin juices around them as you go.

For 4. Heartwarming, glowing red and white, with garlic and tomato.

A couple of thoughts on the lamb belly

- Roast potatoes; very creamy and soft mashed potato; steamed spinach; a handful of arugula dressed with lemon juice.
- Like a pork belly, lamb belly has plenty of fat to keep it juicy as it cooks. It needs a generous amount of seasoning.

An alternative spice rub

Make the rub with 3 tablespoons of smoked paprika, 3 tablespoons of cumin seeds, and 2 tablespoons of garlic salt. Massage into the scored lamb belly, then drizzle with oil and roast as opposite.

Slow-Roast Belly of Lamb

lamb belly, rosemary, yellow mustard seeds, garlic salt, celery seeds, thyme

Preheat the oven to 325°F (170°C). Lay **a lamb belly, weighing about 1½ pounds (700g),** out flat, fat side up, then score with a knife at ⅜-inch (1cm) intervals. Mix together **4 tablespoons of chopped rosemary, 3 tablespoons of yellow mustard seeds, 2 tablespoons of garlic salt, 3 tablespoons of celery seeds,** and **the leaves from 6 small sprigs of thyme,** then rub this mix into the lamb. Drizzle with **olive oil** so the surface is nicely moist, then roast for 1¼ hours. Briefly let the meat rest, then serve in thick slices.

For 4. Savory, juicy. Frugal and aromatic.

Other fillings for the savory Danish

Caramelized onions, Parmesan, capers

Peel and thinly slice onions and cook in butter over low to moderate heat until they are soft and bronze. They should be tender enough to crush between finger and thumb. Stir in grated Parmesan, black pepper, and a few capers. Spread over the pastry as opposite, roll, and bake.

Smoked mackerel, crème fraîche

Mash smoked mackerel with a fork, fastidiously removing any fine bones, season with pepper and lemon juice and maybe a caper or two, then mix to a soft but not sloppy paste with a little crème fraîche. Spread over the rectangle of pastry, roll, and bake.

Sausage Danish

sausages, puff pastry, fennel seeds, egg

Preheat the oven to 400°F (200°C). Lightly flour a pastry board or work surface, then roll out **13 ounces (375g) all-butter puff pastry** to a rectangle about 8 x 12 inches (20 x 30cm).

Remove the casings from **14 ounces (400g) breakfast sausages** (slice the casings from one end to the other, then peel away from the sausage meat). Spread the sausage meat over the pastry, leaving a small border around the edges. Scatter over **2 tablespoons of fennel seeds**. Brush the edges with **a little beaten egg**.

With the long edge facing you, roll the short sides of the pastry, both left and right, until the rolls meet in the middle. Brush with more beaten egg and press the rolls lightly together. Cut into 8 to 10 finger-thick slices. Place these flat on a baking sheet and brush lightly with more egg. Bake for 10 to 15 minutes, till puffed and golden.

Makes 8 to 10. *Viennoiserie* for carnivores.

Some thoughts on the sausages and mash

- Cooking sausages slowly will keep them from splitting and will allow a good sticky coat to develop on their exterior.
- Once the sausages are browned, you can let them finish cooking in the stock.
- After crushing the potatoes with a potato masher, beat them with a wooden spoon to incorporate some air and make them light and fluffy.
- Stir a little whole-grain or smooth Dijon mustard into the gravy at the end.
- Use Madeira or dry Marsala in place of some of the stock.
- Add a couple of sage leaves to the gravy.
- Mushrooms, quartered and fried in a little butter, then stirred into the gravy, would be something to consider, as would a little grated horseradish.

A classic sausages and mash

Lightly brown 6 decent fresh sausages in a little fat or oil in a heavy pan. Push them to one side and cook 2 peeled and quartered onions, broken into layers, on the other side of the pan. Keep the pieces of onion quite large. Once they are deep gold and caramelized, sprinkle a generous dusting of flour on top and allow to brown very lightly. Pour in 1 cup (250ml) rich stock, bring to a boil, season, then simmer for 20 minutes. To make the mash, peel 2 or 3 large potatoes, cut them into large pieces, and boil in lightly salted water or steam them till tender enough to mash. Add a thick slice of butter and beat till light and fluffy. Serve with the sausages and onion gravy.

Sausages, Mash, and Tomato Gravy

sausages, potatoes, tomatoes, shallots, stock, heavy cream, butter

Preheat the oven to 350°F (180°C). Peel **2 large shallots or small onions**, quarter them lengthwise, then put them in a roasting pan with **6 first-class fresh sausages**. Cut **2 beefsteak tomatoes or large vine-ripened tomatoes** into quarters and add to the pan with **4 tablespoons of olive oil**. Bake for an hour, until nicely browned.

Cut **2 large potatoes** into 6 pieces each, without peeling, then boil them in a large pot of salted water till tender. Remove the roasting pan from the oven, place on the stove, and pour in **2 cups (500ml) beef or chicken stock**. Leave to simmer, stirring regularly.

Drain the potatoes and return them to the pan. Add **3½ tablespoons (50g) butter** and mash with a potato masher. Beat in **4 tablespoons of heavy cream** with a wooden spoon and season carefully. Leave over low heat, stirring regularly.

Mash up the tomatoes in the gravy with a fork, stirring to dissolve any roasted pan juices into the sauce. Serve the sausages and gravy over the creamy mash.

For 2. Bolstering food for a cold night.

Cauliflower-Cheese
Baked Potato

baking potatoes, cauliflower, milk, bay leaves,
Parmesan

Prick **4 large starchy potatoes** with a fork or skewer to keep them
from bursting in the oven, then bake at 400°F (200°C) for 50 minutes
to an hour, till the skin is crisp.

Break **a small head of cauliflower** into large florets, put them into
a saucepan with **3 cups (750ml) milk** and **a couple of bay leaves**, and
bring to a boil. Salt lightly, lower the heat, and simmer till tender.
Remove the cauliflower and set aside.

Slice the tops off the potatoes and discard. Scoop out the potato
flesh, leaving a sturdy shell of potato skin. Mash the flesh with a fork,
then stir it into the milk with **1½ cups (150g) grated Parmesan cheese**.
Season generously, stirring well. Return the cauliflower to the sauce,
then pile the mixture into the potato shells, scatter with more grated
Parmesan, and return to the oven for 15 minutes or so, till the filling
is thoroughly hot and the top is pale gold.

For 4. Nannying, frugal. Utter bliss.

Chorizo Potatoes

baking potatoes, chorizo, Manchego

Rinse **2 large starchy baking potatoes**, salt them all over, pierce them here and there with a fork, then bake at 400°F (200°C) for about 45 minutes, till lightly crisp and cooked right through to the center.

In a food processor, coarsely puree **8 ounces (250g) fresh chorizo**, then place in a shallow nonstick pan and fry till sizzling and lightly browned. Slice the top from each potato, then scrape out the flesh into the chorizo pan, setting the empty potato, shells aside. Continue cooking till the potato colors a little.

Chop **3½ ounces (100g) Manchego cheese** and add to the potato and chorizo, then stuff the mixture back into the empty potato shells. Grate a further **1 ounce (25g) Manchego** and scatter over the potatoes, then bake for 10 to 15 minutes.

For 2. A big, bold baked potato for a cold night.

A couple other ideas for asparagus

Asparagus, bacon, Parmesan

Boil a bundle of asparagus and drain, then slice each stalk into 3 or 4 pieces. Cut 4 slices of bacon or pancetta into short strips and fry them in a shallow pan until crisp. Toss the cooked asparagus into the pan, scatter some grated Parmesan on top, and just as the cheese starts to melt, divide between 2 plates.

Asparagus, garlic, soy

Mix together 2 tablespoons of dark soy sauce, 2 tablespoons of mirin, a pinch of sugar, and a little salt. Fry a bunch of slim asparagus spears in a little oil in a wok till tender. Add a finely sliced clove of garlic. When it has turned golden, add the dressing, bubble briefly, and serve.

Asparagus Cannelloni

asparagus, lasagne noodles, béchamel sauce, Parmesan

Preheat the oven to 350°F (180°C). Trim **12 asparagus spears**. Cook **4 fresh lasagne noodles** measuring roughly 4 x 8 inches (10 x 20cm), in plenty of boiling water for 5 minutes, then drain and brush with **a little olive oil**.

Place a lasagna noodle on your work surface, put 3 raw asparagus spears on it, then roll up loosely. Continue with the others, placing them snugly in a baking dish as you go. Pour over **2 cups (500ml) béchamel sauce** (ready-made is fine for this), nicely seasoned.

Bake for 30 minutes, then scatter ½ **cup (50g) grated Parmesan cheese** over the top and return to the oven for 10 minutes, till the sauce is bubbling and the Parmesan is lightly colored.

For 2. Rich. Needs a crisp salad at its side.

A couple of ideas for chorizo

Spicy sausage, soft, floury bun

Split chorizo sausages in half lengthwise, score their cut sides, then grill till soft and sizzling. Split a bun open for each sausage, spread with mayonnaise, and tuck the hot chorizo in together with some crisp salad leaves, such as iceberg lettuce, and watercress.

Sweet potatoes, spicy sausages

Peel and coarsely chop a couple of sweet potatoes. Toss with a peeled and coarsely chopped onion and 2 tablespoons of olive oil. Roast in an oven set at 400°F (200°C) for 30 to 35 minutes, then add 4 chorizo sausages, cut into fat coins, and toss well. Return to the oven for 15 to 20 minutes, till all is brown and sizzling. Serve with a bowl of mayonnaise.

Chorizo and Potatoes

chorizo, new potatoes, shallots,
young carrots

Put **7 ounces (200g) new potatoes** into boiling water and cook until
tender, drain, and slice into thick coins. Preheat the oven to 350°F
(180°C).

Split **4 fresh chorizo sausages** in half, score them on their cut sides,
then place them in a roasting pan with **a couple of large shallots**,
peeled and halved, their layers separated. Add the cooked potatoes
and **5 ounces (150g) small, young carrots**, thinly sliced. Drizzle with
a little oil, then bake for 20 minutes, till sizzling.

For 2. Smoky, sweet, and piquant.

Another lasagne

A creamy chicken lasagne, leftover chicken meat with onions

Soften a couple of onions in melted butter over moderate heat, add leftover chicken meat (or turkey at Christmas), including all the dark meat from under the carcass and the jelly from the roasting pan. Add fresh thyme leaves or tarragon, heavy cream or crème fraîche, and plenty of seasoning. Layer between sheets of cooked lasagne noodles. Finish with grated Parmesan and bake.

Sausage Lasagne

sausages, dried lasagne, cherry tomatoes,
large tomatoes, Dijon mustard, heavy
cream, Parmesan

Split open 1½ **pounds (750g) plump, tasty fresh sausages**, peel off
their casings, and put the sausage meat into a bowl. Rub **a little olive
oil** on the bottom of a small baking dish. Add **sheets of dried, oven-
ready lasagne**, broken into pieces to make them fit roughly into the
dish. Coarsely chop **12 ounces (350g) cherry tomatoes** and distribute
half of them over the lasagne. Cover with half of the sausage meat
and then another layer of lasagne. Add the remaining half of the
tomatoes, then another layer of lasagne and the last of the sausage
meat. Slice **2 large tomatoes** and put them on top.

Stir **a tablespoon of Dijon mustard** into **1 cup (250ml) heavy cream**,
season lightly, then pour over the top. Cover with **grated Parmesan**.
Bake in an oven set at 400°F (200°C) for 45 minutes.

For 4. Rich, luscious, and filling. A dish to keep out the cold.

Some variations on the pasta bake

Change the pasta to suit what you have. With the possible exception of the small soup types, such as orzo, pretty much any variety is suitable for this recipe.

Bucatini with porcini

Soak a handful of dried porcini in warm water for 10 minutes, till they have plumped up. Fold the porcini into the cream and pasta instead of, or along with, the bacon.

With fresh mushrooms

Slice small cremini mushrooms and fry them in a little butter and oil till they are golden and slightly sticky. Season with thyme leaves, salt, and pepper. Use them in the recipe opposite instead of the pancetta. Add a little parsley too, not too finely chopped; it goes well with the mushrooms.

Spaghetti Bake

spaghetti, bacon, garlic, heavy cream,
vegetable stock, Parmesan

Cook **1 pound (500g) spaghetti or bucatini** in fiercely boiling water
till al dente. Drain, cool in a colander under running water, then set
aside. Cut **12 slices of smoked bacon or thinly sliced pancetta** into
finger-thick pieces. Peel and thinly slice **4 cloves of garlic** and cook
with the bacon in a shallow nonstick pan till the bacon is crisp.

Put the drained pasta in a mixing bowl with **1²/₃ cups (400ml) heavy
cream, ¾ cup (200ml) vegetable stock**, the bacon, and garlic, then
season with salt and black pepper. Toss everything together, then
transfer to a baking dish. Scatter the surface with **a good handful of
grated Parmesan** and bake at 350°F (180°C) for about 30 minutes, till
the surface is lightly golden.

For 4. A savory tangle.

Another idea for pork

Pork tenderloin, ponzu dipping sauce

Warm a thin film of oil in a roasting dish, season a pork tenderloin with salt and pepper, then brown it on all sides in the oil. Roast as opposite till the inside is just cooked, then leave to rest. Meanwhile, make a dipping sauce from a mixture of soy sauce, sugar, rice vinegar, finely minced chiles, and ponzu sauce. A few bean sprouts would be fun too. Slice the pork thickly and dunk each piece in the sauce.

Pork with Blood Orange

spare rib chops, blood orange, oyster sauce,
dark soy sauce, sugar, chile sauce, garlic,
oranges, radishes

Preheat the oven to 350°F (180°C). Mix **2 tablespoons of oyster sauce,
a tablespoon of dark soy sauce, a tablespoon of superfine sugar,**
and **a tablespoon of chile sauce.** Stir in **2 crushed cloves of garlic** and
the **finely grated zest of a blood orange.** Place **10 ounces (300g) spare
rib chops** in the marinade and leave for as long as you can before
roasting—an hour if you have it; 5 minutes if not.

Place the pork on a wire rack in a roasting pan, mixing the
marinade with **1¼ cups (300ml) water** in the bottom of the roasting
pan. Put in the oven and leave to cook for 25 to 30 minutes, until
sticky. Remove the chops from the oven and let them rest briefly,
then remove from the pan.

Place the roasting pan over moderate heat, squeeze in the **juice of
a blood orange,** then bring to a boil and let the mixture reduce to a
thick, glossy sauce. Thinly slice **2 oranges** and slice or halve **6 radishes.**
Slice the ribs and serve with the oranges and radishes.

For 2. Sweet, aromatic, sticky pork. Glowing oranges.

A few variations on the toad in the hole

A quick gravy

Soak the dried porcini in 1 cup (250ml) water. Peel and thinly slice
2 medium onions and soften in butter. Add 2 tablespoons of all-
purpose flour, cook for a few minutes, then pour in 1 cup (250ml)
vegetable stock and the porcini soaking water, then add ⅔ cup
(150ml) Marsala. Simmer for 15 to 20 minutes over low heat, then add
a couple of pinches of sugar, plus salt and pepper. Serve with the toad.

An eggplant and feta version

Toss a layer of sliced eggplant in a generous amount of olive oil, with
chopped thyme, a little dried mint if you have it, and a couple of
crushed cloves of garlic. Bake until all is sizzling and soft, then add a
block of feta, crumbled into large pieces, and toss gently. Pour in the
batter opposite and bake as opposite.

Onion and Mushroom Toad in the Hole

shallots, dried porcini, Caerphilly, eggs,
all-purpose flour, milk, whole-grain
mustard, peanut oil, Parmesan

Peel and halve **6 large shallots**. Cook them in a shallow pan, starting
with the flat side down, in **a little butter and oil** over moderate heat.
Leave for about 20 minutes, turning occasionally and letting them
soften till deep golden brown and sticky.

Cut **6 ounces (165g) Caerphilly cheese** into cubes. Soak ½ cup (15g)
dried porcini in cold water for 10 minutes, then drain. Make a batter
by whisking together **2 eggs, ⅔ cup (150ml) milk, ⅔ cup (150ml) water,
1 cup (125g) all-purpose flour, 1 tablespoon of whole-grain mustard,**
and a little salt and pepper.

Pour a thin layer of **peanut oil** into a shallow roasting pan, about
9 x 12 inches (23 x 30cm), then warm in an oven set at 425°F (220°C) till
the oil starts to smoke. Add the sticky onions, the drained porcini,
and Caerphilly, then quickly pour on the batter. Add **a handful of
grated Parmesan** and bake for 25 minutes or so, till risen.

For 4. Utterly savory. Gorgeous.

Potato Wedges with Gorgonzola Sauce

potatoes, Gorgonzola cheese, bacon,
red pepper flakes, smoked paprika,
heavy cream

Scrub **2 pounds (1kg) medium-size starchy potatoes** but don't peel them. Cut each in half lengthwise, then into thick wedges, 3 or 4 to each half. Cook in boiling salted water for 15 minutes, until they are approaching tenderness. Drain and transfer to a roasting pan. Preheat the oven to 400°F (200°C).

Cook **8 slices bacon** in a shallow pan with **a little oil** till very crisp. Transfer to a food processor, add **a tablespoon of red pepper flakes, 4 tablespoons of peanut oil**, and **a tablespoon of smoked paprika**, and process till the mixture resembles very fine crumbs. Sprinkle the crumbs over the potato wedges and toss gently to coat. Bake for an hour or so, till the wedges are crisp and sizzling.

To make the sauce, warm **1 cup (250ml) heavy cream** in a small nonstick saucepan, add **5 ounces (150g) cubed or crumbled Gorgonzola cheese**, and stir gently till the cheese has melted. Drizzle the warm sauce over the wedges or serve as a dip.

For 4. Lively, crunchy, homey, and fun.

Root Vegetable Tangle

potatoes, parsnip, carrots, onion, rosemary,
pumpkin seeds

Preheat the oven to 400°F (200°C). Shave **8 ounces (250g) potatoes,
a large parsnip**, and **2 large carrots** with a vegetable peeler. Peel and
finely slice **an onion** into rings. Toss the potatoes, parsnip, carrots,
and onion in a large mixing bowl with **a heaping tablespoon of
rosemary leaves, 5 tablespoons of olive oil**, and **2 tablespoons
of pumpkin seeds**, then transfer to a baking sheet. Spread out into
a shallow layer. Bake for 20 minutes, till tender and lightly crisp on
the edges.

For 2. A light main course. A side dish for any grilled meat.

Another idea for chicken

Sautéed chicken, porcini, and Marsala

Cut a handful of new potatoes in half lengthwise. Heat a little olive oil in a large pan, add 4 seasoned chicken pieces and the potatoes, and cook until brown and lightly crisp. Add a couple of chopped garlic cloves and color lightly, then add a handful of soaked dried porcini mushrooms and a little chopped rosemary. Pour in a small glass of dry Marsala and simmer, partially covered with a lid, for about 20 minutes, till the chicken is cooked through. For 2.

Chicken Breasts with Taleggio

chicken breasts, Taleggio cheese, Parma ham, sage

Preheat the oven to 350°F (180°C). Slice **2 large chicken breasts** in half horizontally. Arrange the slices snugly on a lightly oiled baking sheet and season with salt and black pepper. Thickly slice **3 ounces (80g) Taleggio cheese** and place on the chicken pieces. Take **4 thin slices of Parma ham** and wrap one around each piece of chicken, tucking a couple of **sage leaves** into each.

Bake for 10 to 15 minutes, till the cheese has started to flow and the chicken is cooked through. Lift carefully from the baking sheet with a spatula to serve.

For 4. A riff. And a good one.

A thought on the chicken pot roast

I use plump, slightly rounded Marcona almonds for this. Rich and sweet, they contribute so much flavor. Whichever type you use, toast them till they are deep gold in color before adding the liquid.

The basic pot roast

Pot roasting is a very simple method: a chicken, or some chicken pieces (or even a pheasant or guinea fowl), a few chopped onions or leeks, some woody herbs, a few pieces of potato maybe, and some liquid—hard cider works well, as does dry vermouth. Seasoning, some garlic perhaps, and then a tight lid. Into the oven for an hour or two while you do something else. A good-natured way of cooking.

Chicken, Sherry, Almond Pot Roast

chicken thighs, new potatoes, salted almonds, fino sherry, chervil

Preheat the oven to 400°F (200°C). Season **4 large chicken thighs**, then brown them as evenly as you can in **a little oil** in a Dutch oven set over moderate heat. Slice **7 ounces (200g) new potatoes** into thick coins and add them to the pan, letting them color lightly. Drop in **⅔ cup (80g) salted almonds**, allow them to brown until they are a deep gold color, then pour in ½ **cup (100ml) fino sherry.** Leave to bubble for a few seconds to burn off the alcohol, then add ½ **cup (100ml) water**, cover with a tightly fitting lid, and roast for 25 minutes. Remove the lid, add **a small handful of chervil**, and serve.

For 2. Deep flavors from a cheap cut. Salty almonds, pale sherry.

Pork Belly, Pistachios, and Figs

pork belly, sausage meat, pistachios, figs

You will need **a piece of pork belly, about 4 pounds (2kg) in weight**, boned and with its skin scored. Put the pork belly skin side up on a chopping board and cut it into 6 equal pieces, then slice each piece in half horizontally.

Put **1 pound (500g) good fresh sausage meat** in a mixing bowl. Coarsely chop **a rounded ¾ cup (100g) shelled pistachios** and add them to the sausage meat, then chop **4 figs** and stir them in. Season thoroughly with salt and pepper, then spread the mixture over the bottom halves of the meat and place them snugly in a roasting pan. Place the reserved halves on top, press firmly, then roast for 20 minutes at 400°F (200°C).

Turn the oven down to 325°F (160°C), add **a further 6 figs**, cut in half, and continue cooking for 1 hour, till all is soft and succulent.

For 6. Rich, sweet, and fruity. A roast for an autumn day.

A thought on the chickpea cakes

It is the interesting texture of these chickpea cakes that makes them such a winner.

Other chickpea winners

Vegetables, chickpeas, and a basil paste. A main-course soup for summer

Finely chop an onion, a stalk of celery, a small leek, and a carrot, then soften in a tablespoon or two of olive oil over moderate heat. They shouldn't be allowed to color. Add a couple of cloves of crushed garlic, then a chopped zucchini. Pour in 4 cups (1 liter) of vegetable stock, add a couple of bay leaves, then add two drained 14-ounce (400g) cans of chickpeas and leave to simmer for about 30 minutes.

Puree a handful of basil leaves with about ½ cup (50g) grated Parmesan and a couple of tablespoons of olive oil. When the vegetables are tender, serve the soup in shallow bowls and stir in the basil and Parmesan paste at the table.

Chickpeas, tomato, spice, and spinach. A thick but light chickpea stew

Coarsely chop an onion and let it soften in olive oil over moderate heat. Add a couple of finely sliced garlic cloves, a finely chopped chile, and 2 teaspoons of garam masala. Continue cooking for a couple of minutes, then introduce a 14-ounce (400g) can of chopped tomatoes and a 14-ounce (400g) can of chickpeas. Pour in about 1¼ cups (300ml) vegetable stock and leave to simmer, with a seasoning of salt and pepper, for about 20 minutes, till rich and thick.

Wash two large handfuls of spinach, shred into wide ribbons, then stir into the chickpea mixture. Once the spinach has wilted, serve in deep bowls with pieces of crusty bread.

Baked Chickpea Cakes

chickpeas, cannellini or pinto beans, paprika,
garam masala, red pepper flakes, chives,
parsley, yogurt, clementine, mint, watercress

Spread **a 14-ounce (400g) can of chickpeas,** drained and rinsed, onto
a baking sheet and dust with **a teaspoon of paprika** and **a teaspoon
of garam masala.** Bake at 350°F (180°C) till hot, lightly crisp, and
fragrant—about 10 minutes. Set aside.

Drain and rinse a second **14-ounce (400g) can of chickpeas** and
a 14-ounce (400g) can of cannellini or pinto beans, then, using a potato
masher, crush both to a coarse puree. Stir in **a pinch of red pepper
flakes, a tablespoon of chopped chives** and **a tablespoon of chopped
parsley,** a grinding of salt and pepper, then the toasted chickpeas.

Form the mixture into 8 balls. Lightly oil a baking sheet or line it
with parchment, place the balls on top, then brush them with **a little
oil.** Bake at 400°F (200°C) for 20 minutes, until crisp outside.

Make a quick sauce by stirring **the zest of a clementine or small
orange** and **a tablespoon of chopped mint** into ¾ cup (200ml) yogurt.
Serve in a bowl with the chickpea balls and **watercress.**

For 4. Crisp cakes, soft inside. Earthy and homey.

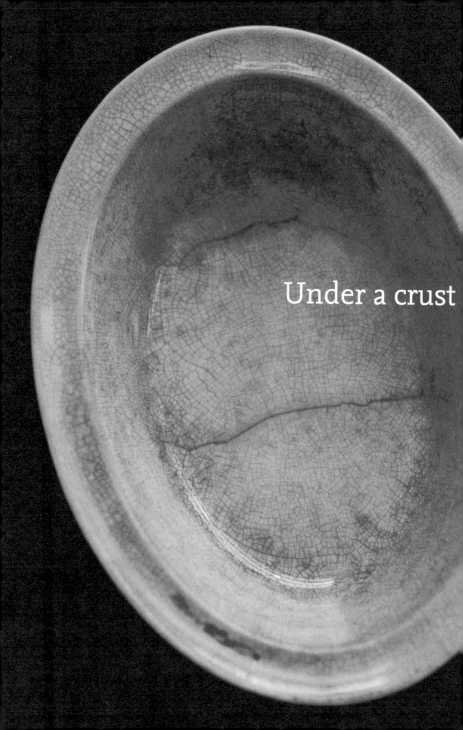

Under a crust

Chop, stir, simmer, cool, roll, shape, cut, fit, fiddle, seal, crimp, glaze, and bake. I love a homemade pie but it's all too much for a weekday. You could use a fluffy potato crust, but then you still have to peel, chop, boil, butter, and mash. It seems too much to ask after a day's work, but sometimes you just want pie.

Even using a shortcut, the crust should flatter the filling. That is why a cheese and onion pasty made with puff pastry works so perfectly, as does a fruit pie made with a soft, sweet crust or a thin dusting of Parmesan cheese on a creamy pasta bake. It need not be pastry, or even potato. Yes, your pie crust can be a piece of frozen puff pastry laid casually over the entire dish, like a duvet slightly too big for the bed, but it can also be grated root vegetables made crisp with butter. It can be thin slices of potato laid over the surface like cobbles, or even a thick layer of thoughtfully seasoned bread crumbs. All that matters is the contrast between crust and filling.

I use store-bought puff pastry without apology; it can give me a nicely crusted beef pie within an hour or so. If you need to, the trick is to take it from freezer to fridge first thing, before you go to work. Seasoned bread crumbs are useful too and can be made in a food processor or blender at the click of a switch. More organized cooks than myself probably keep some in their freezer. A crust in seconds. They are perfect for a cream-rich corn pie but also for a pasta and crab bake. A smashed tortilla can work too, though is probably best crowning a filling it feels at home with, such as some sort of bean stew.

The pies in this chapter have crusts made from cheese, bread crumbs, pastry, root vegetables, and tortilla, and the fillings of fish, beef, vegetables, beans, and pasta are made from scratch. But it is worth giving a thought to using up leftovers by turning them into a pie. The remains of a vegetable casserole such as a ratatouille can be bolstered with a crumb crust, or a little bit of stew left from the previous night topped with a pastry lid. The crust makes the leftovers go further, lends them a heartiness, and gives them a new life.

Yes, a little more time than chucking chicken pieces in a wok but, as I said, sometimes you just want pie.

A few favorites

A crust of hash browns

Coarsely grate a large potato, then peel and thinly slice an onion. Melt a thick slice of butter in a shallow pan, add the potato and onion, and let them cook for 10 minutes or so, till they color slightly. Scatter over a chicken or beef casserole and bake till the crust is golden and crisp.

A Cheddar and crouton crust

Cut thick slices of bread into cubes, discarding the crust, and toss them in a generous quantity of olive oil. Cut thick slices of Cheddar, Gruyère, or other firm, nicely sharp cheese and toss with the bread. Pile in one layer on top of the filling and brown in the oven. You should get crisp croutons floating in little pools of melted cheese. Particularly suited to a vegetable pie.

A parsnip and horseradish crust

Peel and coarsely grate 10 ounces (300g) parsnips and add 3 heaping tablespoons of finely grated fresh horseradish. Melt 3½ tablespoons (50g) of butter in a shallow pan, toss the parsnip in the butter till it starts to soften, place on top of a beef casserole or stew, and bake for 2 hours in an oven set at 325°F (160°C).

A cloud of yellow mash

Peel, boil, and mash parsnips with butter and a little grated nutmeg and black pepper. Pile on top of your filling in large, cloud-like spoonfuls. Avoid the temptation to smooth the surface.

Slow-Cooked Beef Pie with Celery Root Rösti Crust

cubed beef, baby carrots, baby parsnips, garlic, flour, butter, beef or vegetable stock, celery root, fresh horseradish

Season then brown **1 pound (500g) moderately sized cubes of beef** in a little oil in a pan set over moderate heat, then add **7 ounces (200g) whole, short, young carrots** and **3½ ounces (100g) whole young parsnips** and let them brown lightly. Peel and lightly squash **6 cloves of garlic** and add them to the pan, then, as they color, add **2 tablespoons of flour**. Continue cooking till the flour has colored, then stir in **2 cups (500ml) beef or vegetable stock** and simmer for 10 minutes. Transfer the filling to a small pie dish.

Peel and coarsely grate **10 ounces (300g) celery root**, add **3 heaping tablespoons of finely grated fresh horseradish**, then **3½ tablespoons (50g) melted butter**. Toss together gently, place on top of the beef filling, and bake for 1¼ to 1½ hours in an oven set at 325°F (160°C). Steamed kale on the side.

For 4 to 6. Pie, but with a crisp, grated vegetable crust. Earthy, mild, wholesome.

Some thoughts on the salmon pie

- A summer dish.
- Without the cream, the dish tastes fresher but somehow less interesting.
- You could punch up the heat with a teaspoon of bottled green peppercorns.
- To the opposite recipe add a couple of handfuls of cooked, shelled mussels.
- Swap the cod for scallops to make a richer, more "special occasion" pie.
- If cucumber isn't your thing, try button mushrooms that you have first cooked in butter.
- Change the dill to tarragon, chopping the leaves quite finely.
- This pie is wonderful with leeks in it (in place of the cucumber). Slice the leeks, then sauté them in butter, covered with a lid or a piece of parchment paper. They will soften and sweeten.

Salmon and Cucumber Pie

salmon, cod, shrimp, cucumber, cream,
capers, bread, butter, dill, lemon

Preheat the oven to 350°F (180°C). Process **3 ounces (85g) white bread**
in a food processor with **a handful of dill** and the **grated zest of a
lemon**. Peel, seed, and chop **a medium cucumber**.

Remove the skin from **10 ounces (300g) salmon fillet** and **7 ounces
(200g) cod fillet**, cut into large chunks, and put in a shallow baking dish
with **8 ounces (250g) raw, shelled shrimp**. Tuck in the cucumber. Sprinkle
in **a teaspoon of capers**. Season and add **3½ tablespoons (50g) butter** in
pieces, ⅔ **cup (150ml) heavy cream**, and then scatter over the crumb
topping. Bake in the oven for 25 minutes. Serve with peas. Spoonfuls of
fresh green peas!

For 4. A light, unfussy fish pie for a summer's day.

A couple of thoughts on the potpie

- There is some very good all-butter puff pastry around, and it's worth keeping a sheet of it in your freezer. A stew becomes a pie in a heartbeat.
- The filling should be cold before you lay the pastry on top, but I have gotten away with using it while warm. Life isn't always perfect.

For a change

Chicken breasts, Madeira, the luxury of heavy cream

Flatten 2 chicken breasts by wrapping them in plastic wrap and hitting them with a rolling pin or meat mallet, then dust them in a little seasoned flour. Melt a thick slice of butter in a shallow pan, add the chicken, then cook briefly on both sides till golden. Lift out the chicken, add a glass of Madeira to the pan, then bubble and stir to dissolve any chicken bits that have been left behind in the pan. When the liquid has reduced to half its original quantity, stir in 4 tablespoons of heavy cream, season, and simmer briefly.

Quick Chicken Potpie

chicken, onions, mushrooms, white beer,
all-butter puff pastry, stock, tarragon

Peel and coarsely chop **2 onions**. Brown **14 ounces (400g) diced chicken**
in **a little oil**, remove, then add the chopped onions and **3½ ounces
(100g) quartered mushrooms**, letting them brown. Add **3 tablespoons
of flour** and continue cooking for about 5 minutes. Then add **1⅓ cups
(330ml) white beer** and **1¼ cups (300ml) chicken or vegetable stock** and
bring to a boil. Lower the heat, then add **4 tablespoons of chopped
tarragon leaves** and a grinding of salt and pepper and simmer for
about 10 minutes, till thick. Transfer to a baking dish and leave to cool
for as long as you can.

Put **a ready-rolled all-butter puff pastry sheet** on a work surface
and, using the dish as a template, cut out a disk to fit the top. Lay the
pastry disk gently on top of the sauce, then cut three slits with the
point of a knife. Decorate with the remaining pastry, cut into leaves
or whatever you fancy. Bake at 350°F (180°C) for 30 minutes.

For 4. Sometimes, you just want pie.

More mac and cheese ideas

The classic

A classic macaroni cheese recipe is made with about 8 ounces (250g)
cooked short macaroni and a good 2 cups (500ml) béchamel sauce.
I add about ½ cup (75g) grated cheese (whatever kind needs using up)
to the sauce and top it with a generous scattering of grated Parmesan.

Blue cheese mac

To a classic mac and cheese recipe (made with either a rich béchamel
sauce, grated Cheddar and Parmesan, or a contemporary version with
crème fraîche, fontina, and Parmesan), add a soft, ripe blue cheese,
such as Gorgonzola.

Leek macaroni cheese

To a traditional cheese-sauce-style recipe, add a stirring of sliced leeks
that you have cooked very slowly in a generous amount of butter
without allowing them to color.

Crab Mac and Cheese

crabmeat, pasta, milk, heavy cream,
Dijon mustard, whole-grain mustard,
bread crumbs, Parmesan

Preheat the oven to 350°F (180°C). Boil **8 ounces (250g) medium-size pasta, such as penne, serpentelli, or macaroni**, in a large pot of well-salted boiling water for about 9 minutes, till tender. Drain and return to the saucepan, then add **1²⁄₃ cups (400ml) milk, 1 cup (250ml) heavy cream, a tablespoon of Dijon mustard**, and **2 tablespoons of whole-grain mustard** and bring to a boil. Lower the heat, stir in **10 ounces (300g) lump crabmeat**, and simmer gently, stirring often, for about 5 minutes.

Check the seasoning, then transfer to a deep baking dish. Mix **½ cup (25g) fresh white bread crumbs** with **¼ cup (25g) grated Parmesan cheese**, scatter on top, and bake for 20 minutes, till bubbling around the edges.

For 4. Rich, sweet, and unctuous.

You can tweak a corn pie deliciously

• To the recipe opposite add blanched broccoli, cut into large florets.
• Drop the bacon and use cooked sausage instead, or shredded salami.
• Use canned beans, such as cannellini or navy beans, drained of their
  liquid, in place of half the corn. The dish is not as sweet this way but
  is even more substantial.

Or make a corn fritter

Make little corn fritters by draining a can of corn, putting it into a bowl,
then adding a couple of beaten egg yolks, some salt and black pepper,
and enough flour to make a heavy batter. Beat the two egg whites to a
stiff froth, then fold into the corn mixture. Heat butter in a frying pan
until sizzling, then drop large spoonfuls of the batter into the pan and
cook till golden on the underside. Turn with a thin spatula, cook the
other side, and drain briefly on paper towels before eating.

Corn Crumb-Crust Pie

canned corn, onion, potatoes, bacon, milk,
heavy cream, parsley, bread crumbs, butter

Preheat the oven to 350°F (180°C). Peel and slice **an onion** and let
it soften in **2 tablespoons (30g) butter** over moderate heat. Cut
12 ounces (350g) potatoes into quite small cubes and add them to
the pan, then cut **8 slices of bacon** into pieces the size of a postage
stamp and stir into the onions and potatoes. When the potatoes are
tender, add ¾ **cup (200ml) milk** and ¾ **cup (200ml) heavy cream** to
the pan with **two 10-ounce (300g) cans of corn** and continue cooking
for 10 minutes.

To make the crust, in a shallow pan melt **3½ tablespoons (50g)
butter** over moderate heat, then mix in **a large handful of chopped
parsley** and **1½ cups (80g) fresh bread crumbs** and leave to color
lightly.

Transfer the corn mixture to an oven dish, scatter over the bread
crumb crust, and bake for 20 minutes.

For 4. Sweet crunch and cream.

A couple of other ideas for kale

Bacon fat, kale, and juniper

Heat some bacon fat or ibérico fat—or, if you must, olive oil—in a
large pan, then use it to cook a sliced onion. Add a sprig or two of
thyme, some lightly crushed juniper berries, a glass of sparkling
wine—nothing too extravagant—then add shredded kale and stir
briefly before covering with a lid and simmering for 10 minutes.
As the kale becomes tender, add salt and pepper. An uplifting dish
to accompany a pork-based main course.

Kale bruschetta

Remove the tough stems from the kale. Simmer the leaves in
chicken stock for 10 to 15 minutes, till soft and dark, then drain
and set both stock and kale aside. Have ready some rounds of hot,
toasted sourdough bread. Rub the bread with a cut clove of young
garlic, place in a shallow bowl, then spoon over a little of the hot
stock. Add the cooked kale, drizzle with fruity, verdant green olive
oil, and finish with a mean squeeze of lemon and coarse flakes of
sea salt.

Gratin of Kale
and Almonds

kale, sliced almonds, red onions, cream,
béchamel sauce, Parmesan

Preheat the oven to 400°F (200°C). Peel and finely slice **2 red onions**.
Warm **a little peanut or canola oil** in a shallow pan, then add the
onions and fry till soft and, here and there, pale gold. Remove the
tender leaves from **14 ounces (400g) kale** and chop the coarse stems.
Add the chopped stems to the onions and continue cooking till the
kale has softened and brightened. Add the kale leaves and stir, cooking
for only a couple of minutes, then add ¼ **cup (25g) sliced almonds**.

Transfer the onion and kale mixture to an ovenproof dish, stir
1¼ **cups (300ml) heavy cream** into **2 cups (500ml) béchamel sauce**
(ready-made is fine) with **a good handful of grated Parmesan**, then
check the seasoning. Pour over the kale and onion, then scatter with
a little more Parmesan and **a further** ¼ **cup (25g) sliced almonds**.
Bake for 30 minutes, till golden and bubbling.

For 4. A vegetable. A cheese and cream sauce. The crunch of almonds.

Pinto Beans, Chorizo, and Tortilla

chorizo, pinto beans, corn tortillas,
sun-dried tomatoes, onion, garlic, Cheddar

Slice **1 pound (450g) fresh chorizo sausages** into short lengths. Drain
a scant cup (100g) sun-dried tomatoes (but keep the oil) and chop
them coarsely. Fry the sausage in a shallow pan with 4 tablespoons
of the oil from the sun-dried tomatoes. Peel and slice **an onion**, add
to the pan, and cook for 10 minutes, till the onion softens, then add
a crushed clove of garlic. Drain **a 14-ounce (400g) can of pinto beans**
and add them to the pan. Season, then transfer to a baking dish.

Tear **4 corn tortillas** into pieces, toss with the sun-dried tomatoes,
and scatter over the beans followed by **6 tablespoons of grated
Cheddar**. Bake for 10 minutes at 400°F (200°C). Serve with an
avocado salad.

For 4. Filling, earthy, and fun.

In a wok

In some ways, this is the most exciting kind of quick cooking—at least if the wok is hot enough. The moment the food goes into the pan, there should be a slight sense of danger and fun. Of sizzle and spit, crackle and hiss. There may even, very briefly, be a flame or two. If your heart doesn't beat just a little faster when you start stir-frying, then your wok just ain't hot enough.

Get a thin wok. I use mine mostly for stir-fries, or occasionally for steaming a small fish. The crucial thing is that the steel should be thin. The food needs to sizzle on the hot metal and cook very quickly, which is why we must cut it small. At one time the stir-fry was best left to professionals, but now that home gas stoves are more powerful, we can do it successfully at home.

Although this method of cooking fits neatly into the premise of this book, it should be said that it is only the cooking time that is minimal. The preparation will almost certainly take longer than the cooking. A stir-fry of vegetables, for instance, must include the time to peel and shred the ginger and finely chop the garlic and green onion. The vegetables need to be cut into small pieces or thin slices. Any large chunks will slow down the cooking process, the food will steam rather than fry, and your stir-fry will no longer live up to its name.

This remains one of my favorite methods of cooking. I like the speed at which the food browns and the whole sense of fun you get with high-temperature frying. Above all, I love my woks. I have two: a shallow Japanese iron pot with short handles that I use for meals for one (and I suspect is not really a wok at all) and a vast, black Chinese thing from Chinatown that I have had for a decade or more. Both harness incredible heat.

You can cook Thai food in a wok—I have often made a green curry in mine—and woks are probably more versatile than they are given credit for. But they are principally for food that needs exceptionally high heat and constant movement around the searing-hot sides of the pan. The clue is in the word *stir-fry*.

A few favorites

Chicken, mushrooms, and beans

Skin a large chicken breast, cut it into thick slices, and marinate in a tablespoon each of rice wine and light soy sauce for about 15 minutes. Heat a little peanut oil in a wok and, just as it starts to smoke lightly, toss in 2 chopped cloves of garlic and a handful of sliced cremini mushrooms. Fry and stir, briefly and quickly, over high heat. Stir a dusting of cornstarch into the chicken, then add to the pan and continue frying for a couple of minutes. At the last minute, add a handful of raw green beans, cut into short lengths. Stir in a tablespoon of light soy sauce, a little toasted sesame oil, and a little pepper. Serve with rice.

Smoked salmon, wasabi

Add beaten eggs to a little fizzing butter, stir with chopsticks, then add folds of smoked salmon, a spoonful of crème fraîche, and a dash of wasabi or a few bottled green peppercorns.

Fried shrimp, tomato sauce

Into a blender or food processor put a small, coarsely chopped onion, a seeded medium-hot chile, a couple of tomatoes, a tablespoon of light soy sauce, and 3 tablespoons of ketchup, then puree to a thick sauce.

In a wok, heat 2 tablespoons of oil, then fry 2 finely chopped garlic cloves for a few seconds, until they are golden. Then add 2 or 3 large handfuls of peeled raw shrimp and fry for 3 or 4 minutes, until they are lightly golden. Stir in the tomato sauce and let it sizzle for a minute or two. Finish with chopped cilantro.

Stir-Fried Chicken with Cashews and Broccoli

chicken breasts, salted cashews,
broccolini, five-spice powder, garlic

Remove the skin from **2 large chicken breasts**, then slice the
flesh into thick chunks. Put the chicken into a bowl and toss with
1 tablespoon of five-spice powder. Thinly slice **2 garlic cloves**, add
to the chicken, and toss together gently.

Heat **2 tablespoons of peanut oil** in a wok, then add the spiced
chicken pieces and fry for a couple of minutes, till golden. Add **⅓ cup
(50g) salted cashews, 7 ounces (200g) broccolini**, and **¾ cup (200ml) hot
water** and bring to a boil. Cover with a lid and steam for a couple of
minutes, till the greens are tender. You will need a spoon for the juices.

For 2. Crisp greens, crunchy cashews, tender chicken.

Note: You can thicken the juices of a stir-fry by adding cornstarch
or arrowroot. I prefer not to, unless I am making a classic dish that
requires it. If you like a thicker sauce, add a couple of teaspoons
of Shaoxing wine and 2 tablespoons of cornstarch along with the
five-spice as you toss the chicken.

A few thoughts on the shrimp and noodles

- The choice of noodles is vast. I tend to use a quick rice noodle for this recipe—either the wok-ready sort or those that require only a short soak in boiling water. Up to you.
- Whether you use cooked or raw shrimp, they need cooking for only a couple of minutes. Once a raw shrimp has gone from gray to pink, it is cooked. Frozen shrimp must be defrosted before use.

For a change

The otherworldliness of squid, the homeyness of udon noodles

Use a wider noodle, such as the fat udon. Crush a couple cloves of garlic with the green onions in the recipe opposite. Slice a squid into rings and add to the pan. Toss with the noodles, plus chopped cilantro, mint, Thai basil—whatever you fancy. A stir-fry of green and white.

Pure, clear chicken noodle soup

Peel a thumb-size piece of fresh ginger and cut it into matchsticks. Bring 4 cups (1 liter) of chicken stock to a boil, add the ginger, and simmer briskly for 5 minutes. Drop 5 ounces (150g) dried noodles into the stock and cook for 3 or 4 minutes, till almost tender. Lift them out with tongs and drop into 2 wide bowls. Add a tablespoon of oyster sauce and 2 tablespoons of light soy sauce to the stock, followed by a couple of small, sweet green onions, very finely sliced. Simmer for a minute or two longer, then ladle it over the noodles. Shake in a few drops of sesame oil before eating.

Shrimp, Noodles, and Spring Carrots

shrimp, noodles, carrots, green onions,
chile, ginger, orange juice, dark soy sauce,
fish sauce

Scrub **7 ounces (200g) spring carrots** and slice them in half
lengthwise. Steam or boil them for 7 to 8 minutes, till tender but not
soft. Drain and set aside. Soak **5 ounces (150g) noodles** according to
the instructions on the package.

Finely slice **3 green onions**. Halve lengthwise and seed **a medium-
size chile**, then slice it finely. Peel and grate **a knob of fresh ginger**.
Heat **a tablespoon of peanut oil** in a wok, then add the green onions,
ginger, and chile and fry quickly, tossing and stirring for a few minutes.
Add **7 ounces (200g) peeled raw shrimp**. As soon as the shrimp show
signs of changing color, add the carrots. Drop in the noodles, then
pour in **½ cup (125ml) orange juice, a tablespoon of dark soy sauce**,
and **a tablespoon of fish sauce**. Sizzle and serve.

For 2. Sweet and gentle.

A couple of seafood variations on the pork and cucumber

Crab, cabbage, yuzu

Finely shred red and white cabbage, then soak in cold water to crisp up. Make a citrus mayonnaise by stirring a few teaspoons of yuzu juice (available from Japanese food stores) into mayonnaise, to taste. Toss the drained and dried cabbage with fresh lump crabmeat, the yuzu mayonnaise, and a little chopped cilantro.

Squid, pea shoots, and arugula

Toss hot grilled squid with whole cilantro and mint leaves, arugula leaves, and pea shoots. Dress with lime juice, fish sauce, a pinch of sugar, and a little chopped red chile.

Aromatic Pork with Cucumber

pork belly, cucumber, dried shallots, garlic, toasted sesame oil, ginger, sugar, mirin, lime

Puree **3 tablespoons of dried shallots** with **2 peeled cloves of garlic, 2 tablespoons of toasted sesame oil, a tablespoon of grated fresh ginger**, and **2 teaspoons of sugar**. Transfer to a bowl. Cut **10 ounces (300g) boned pork belly** into thin slices and toss with the pureed aromatics. Lightly peel **a cucumber** and thickly slice into chunky matchsticks. Sprinkle with **2 tablespoons of mirin**.

Heat a wok, add **a thin film of peanut oil**, add the pork, and cook for a few minutes till nicely crisp, then add **a tablespoon of lime juice**. Toss briefly with the cucumber and eat immediately.

For 2. Aromatic, sizzling pork. The crunch of cucumber.

Some thoughts on the pork

- Without the crisp lettuce and a cold beer, the dish will be too salty. They are as much part of the recipe as the pork.
- Cubes of pork from the shoulder or leg, lean and firm, are more suited to stir-frying than a fattier cut. Save fat-rich cuts for slow cooking where the fat has time to moisten and enrich the meat.
- Move the ingredients quickly around the pan so the pepper doesn't burn. Use canola or peanut oil, which has a lower flashpoint at high temperatures than olive oil.
- If Sichuan peppercorns prove evasive, you can still make a simple salt 'n' pepper pork without them. It will simply be less aromatic. Include a chopped clove of garlic or 4 chopped green onions if you wish, or a grated knob of ginger or galangal. A grating of lemon zest at the end will freshen the flavors and work well with the black pepper.
- Coarsely grated carrot, cut as if for remoulade, would be an idea with the pork, as would a few green beans. Cilantro leaves, or fresh mint, are appropriate here too, as is picking the hot meat up with a piece of warm, soft flatbread or romaine lettuce.

Salt and Pepper Pork

cubed pork, Sichuan peppercorns, black peppercorns, sea salt flakes, lettuce, mint, cilantro

Finely crush **a tablespoon of black peppercorns** and **a tablespoon of Sichuan peppercorns** using a pestle and mortar or some other heavy weight, then toss with **1 pound (500g) cubed pork shoulder or leg**. Set aside for 20 minutes or so. Heat a wok or large frying pan over high heat. When the pan is very hot, pour in **2 tablespoons of canola or peanut oil** and swirl around the pan. As soon as it starts to shimmer and smoke slightly, add the pork together with **a tablespoon of sea salt flakes**. Fry at a high temperature, stirring regularly for 5 minutes or so, till the meat has colored here and there. Transfer a warm bowl and serve with **iceberg lettuce** and maybe **a few mint or cilantro leaves**. Ice-cold beer to drink.

For 2. Mouth-popping salty heat. Cool, crisp lettuce.

Pork Belly with Lime and Sichuan Peppercorns

pork belly, Sichuan peppercorns, honey, lime,
fresh noodles, chives

Cut **10 ounces (300g) boned pork belly** into cubes about 1¼ inches (3cm)
thick. Heat **2 tablespoons of peanut oil** in a wok, then, when the oil
is very hot, add the meat. Brown quickly, then add **2 tablespoons
of coarsely ground Sichuan peppercorns**, shortly followed by
2 tablespoons of honey and **the juice of 2 limes**. Continue cooking,
moving the meat around the pan for a couple of minutes, then add
7 ounces (200g) thick, soft fresh noodles and **4 tablespoons of
chopped chives**. Let the noodles warm and the chives mellow and
soften, then season and eat.

For 2. Sweet, sharp, luscious. The peace of noodles.

Another homey option

Miso, mushroom, and beef broth

Dissolve 3 tablespoons of dark red (aka) miso in 4 cups (1 liter) of boiling water. Pour into a saucepan, add 3½ ounces (100g) fresh enoki mushrooms, 2 red bird's eye chiles, halved, and a tablespoon of dark soy sauce. Simmer for a couple of minutes, until the mushrooms are soft and have a slightly jellied texture. Pour into 2 deep bowls and add a small handful of cilantro leaves to each. Serve piping hot, with 3½ ounces (100g) raw filet mignon, rump, or rib-eye beef, sliced paper-thin, dipping the slices into the broth for a few seconds before eating. Serve with soup spoons for the broth.

Light, umami-rich broth, tender beef. A bowl to restore, heal, and warm. For 2.

Soba Noodles, Salmon, and Shrimp

soba noodles, salmon, shrimp, chile, dark soy sauce, fish sauce, chives, cilantro

Bring a large pan of water to a boil. Salt the water generously, add **7 ounces (200g) dry soba noodles**, and boil for 6 minutes. (Ignore the package instructions, because the noodles will get a bit more cooking later.) Drain and cool under running water.

Cut **1 pound (450g) salmon fillet** into finger-thick strips. Finely slice **a red chile** but leave the seeds in—you want a little heat in this dish. Put a large wok over a very hot flame, leave for a second or two, pour in **1 tablespoon of peanut oil**, swirl it around, then add the salmon and **8 ounces (250g) large, raw peeled shrimp**. Add the finely sliced chile. Drop in the partially cooked noodles, then continue to stir and fry. The salmon may break up a bit but no matter.

Add **a tablespoon of dark soy sauce** and **a tablespoon of fish sauce**, **2 tablespoons of chopped chives**, and **a handful of torn cilantro**, sizzle briefly, and serve.

For 4. Homey noodles, luxurious seafood.

A couple of variations on the wasabi beef

Sirloin, garlic, and zucchini

Try filet mignon or sirloin steak, prepared as in the recipe opposite, but with zucchini cut into matchsticks instead of the snow peas. This is good with a little sliced garlic added with the mushrooms.

Steak and greens

Steak as opposite (or use skirt or chuck steak, if you wish), but use button mushrooms, cut in half to give juicy little nuggets, then add shredded spring greens instead of snow peas. A juicy, messy tangle.

Wasabi Miso Beef

sirloin steak, wasabi paste, white miso,
Japanese mushrooms, snow peas

Heat **a little peanut oil** in a wok. Add **a 10-ounce (300g) sirloin steak**,
in one piece, and let it brown nicely on both sides. Remove the steak
and leave to rest. Add **4 ounces (110g) small Japanese mushrooms
(shimeji or enoki)** to the pan and move them around as they fry so
they pick up all the juices from the steak. Finely shred **7 ounces (200g)
snow peas**, add to the pan, and fry for a minute. Add **2 tablespoons of
white (shiro) miso, 2 teaspoons of wasabi paste**, and ½ **cup (100ml)
water**. Continue to fry and stir briefly. Cut the steak into pencil-thick
slices and return them to the pan for a minute or so, keeping the
center of the meat rare.

For 2. The savor of steak, the refreshing crunch of snow peas.

On a plate

I cannot count the times dinner has been a collection of things on a plate. An assembly of ingredients that work together but are not what you could call a "dish." It could be as simple as good bread and Cheddar; a salad of ripe, pepper-dusted tomatoes and cool mozzarella; a plate of salami with a jagged piece of airy ciabatta or a store-bought pâté with hot toast. And talking of toast, my dinner has been that many a time, albeit with a few flat mushrooms cooked in garlic butter on top or perhaps a can of beans gussied up with a bit of chile. (Others would no doubt mention boiled eggs, tomatoes, or eggs scrambled into a fluffy cloud.)

The assembly can also come in the form of a salad. Of cucumber and tuna perhaps; beets and air-dried ham; or a sharp apple salad with feta cheese. It may be an artfully arranged mixture of fennel and ricotta, or something with a cooked element such as bulgur wheat with figs and maybe a slice or two of Parma ham on the side.

Stuff that goes pretty much straight onto the plate often includes a raw ingredient at its heart—something so perfect you want to eat it in all its glory. Fresh crab, cool and salty; a quivering ball of milky-white mozzarella; peas from the garden tossed with ham.

These are, by their nature, light meals. A lunch, a quick bite after work before you go out, a simple supper. I value them for their immediacy and lack of fuss. They are instant hits that involve almost no cooking. Dinner without turning on the oven.

Tomatoes, sun-dried tomatoes, feta, balsamic vinegar, basil. Gentle flavors for when you are out of sorts

Pour 1 cup (200g) couscous into a bowl, pour over enough boiling water to cover, then leave for 10 minutes or so, till the grain has soaked up the water.

Marinate a single 8-ounce (250g) piece of feta in 2 tablespoons of olive oil and 2 tablespoons of balsamic vinegar for 20 minutes. Chop 10 ounces (300g) cherry tomatoes and ½ cup (50g) sun-dried tomatoes (the ones that come in oil) and mix them together in a bowl. Crumble the feta into large pieces, then fork them through the grains with the tomatoes and 3 heaping tablespoons of chopped basil leaves. For 4.

Basil, pine nuts, garlic, mozzarella, and lemon-scented olives

Heat 1 cup (250ml) tomato juice with a crushed clove of garlic, then pour it over ⅔ cup (125g) couscous and cover. Leave for 10 minutes, then fluff the grains gently with a fork.

Make an herb oil by pureeing ½ cup (100ml) olive oil with ⅔ cup (15g) basil leaves in a blender or food processor. Coarsely dice or tear a 4-ounce (125g) ball of buffalo mozzarella. Chop a green onion, a couple of plump, ripe tomatoes, and a large handful of parsley and mix with 1 cup (125g) lemon-marinated olives, sliced in half. Toast a handful of pine nuts and chop them. Toss together the mozzarella, parsley, green onion, tomatoes, and olives, then fold in the fluffed couscous and drizzle with the basil oil. For 2 to 3.

A crisp accompaniment to ham

Carrot and celery root make good partners in a remoulade, the carrot introducing a little sweetness to the mineral qualities of the celery root. Peel a celery root and 2 or 3 carrots, then shred them into matchsticks about 2½ inches (6cm) long. Salt lightly, then toss with a little lemon juice to stop the roots from browning. Toss with crème fraîche, Dijon mustard, and a dash of wasabi paste. Yes, wasabi paste. Wonderful with slices of air-dried ham.

More tuna salads

Tuna, eggplant, basil, and lemon

Cut a large eggplant into large dice and cook slowly in olive oil in
a shallow pan. When it is golden and silkily soft, add 2 finely sliced
garlic cloves and continue cooking for a couple of minutes, till the
garlic starts to color. Add a handful of chopped basil and chives.
Drain a 6-ounce (160g) can of tuna, gently break up the tuna, and
stir it into the eggplant. Squeeze over the juice of a lemon. Boil
10 ounces (300g) spaghetti in a pot of generously salted water for
9 minutes. Toss the sauce lightly with the drained pasta. For 4.

Tuna and tomato bruschetta

Toast some sourdough bread and, while it is hot, pile onto it a few slices
of ripe tomato, a handful of tuna, and a spoonful of salsa verde made in
the blender (olive oil, lemon juice, arugula, basil, parsley, anchovy,
capers, no garlic).

Tuna and Cucumber Salad

tuna, new potatoes, cucumber, Dijon mustard, dill, olives, white wine vinegar, sugar

Wipe **8 ounces (240g) new potatoes** clean, removing any loose flakes of skin, then boil them in plenty of salted water till just tender. Lightly peel **a medium-size cucumber**, cut it in half lengthwise, then scrape out the seeds and pulp from the center with a teaspoon, reserving them for the dressing. Cut the cucumber into finger-thick chunks and place in a large mixing bowl.

Make the dressing: Put **a mere pinch of superfine sugar** in a blender or food processor, add **a tablespoon of white wine vinegar, a tablespoon of Dijon mustard**, a little salt and pepper, and the reserved seeds and pulp from the cucumber. Pour in **a tablespoon of olive oil** and puree briefly to a smooth, creamy dressing. Pour the dressing onto the cucumber, add **2 tablespoons of chopped dill**, and stir gently.

Drain the potatoes, then cut each one into about 4 thick coins. Add the warm potatoes to the cucumber, along with **4 ounces (125g) best-quality drained canned tuna in olive oil**, turning them over carefully in the dressing so they are evenly coated. Scatter over **a handful of purple niçoise olives**.

For 2. A light main dish. The usefulness of a can of tuna.

A few thoughts on the mackerel and peas

• Whole smoked mackerel are often juicier than fillets.
• You could use fava beans instead of edamame.

For when meat is what you want

Surf 'n' turf

Add a little bacon, cut into postage-stamp-size pieces, to the green onion. Smoked meats work well with oily seafood such as salmon and mackerel.

Smoked Mackerel with Peas and Edamame

smoked mackerel, peas, edamame, ciabatta, green onion

Cook **7 ounces (200g) edamame beans in their pods** in lightly salted boiling water for 10 minutes. Drain the beans and pop them out of the pods. Cook **1 cup (150g) frozen peas** in a large pot of boiling water till tender, then drain. Flake **10 ounces (300g) smoked mackerel** into large pieces. Tear **3½ ounces (100g) ciabatta bread** into large pieces and fry them in **3 tablespoons of olive oil** in a shallow nonstick pan over moderate heat till pale gold and crisp. Chop **a green onion** and add to the pan, then toss in the edamame and peas, followed by the smoked mackerel. Serve immediately.

For 2 to 3. A smoky, green feast.

More bright and crunchy salads

- Raw cauliflower florets, sliced thickly, tossed with cooked shrimp, dill, mayonnaise, and small pieces of lemon flesh.
- Pears, sliced and tossed with air-dried ham, then dressed with cider vinegar, whole-grain mustard, and lemon juice.
- Green mango, peeled, pitted, and sliced, then tossed with coarsely shredded cucumber, green onion, radish, mint, cilantro, lime juice, and a dash of sesame oil.
- Shredded roast chicken, chopped peanuts, bean sprouts, finely sliced red chile, mint leaves, and shredded carrot, tossed with a dressing made from equal amounts of mirin, lime juice, and fish sauce, sweetened with a pinch of sugar.

Apple, Ginger, and Endive

apples, ginger, endive, limes, cider vinegar, feta, sprouts

Squeeze the juice from **2 ripe, slightly yellowing limes**. Finely grate into it **2 teaspoons of fresh ginger**, then stir in **a tablespoon of cider vinegar**.

Thinly slice **2 sweet apples**, then put them straight into the dressing. Tear up **2 endive**. Toss with the apple, **a handful of sprouts**, and the dressing. Serve with a huge wedge of **feta cheese**.

For 4 as a side dish. Fresh, ultracrisp, almost astringent. A dish to awaken the senses.

Other iterations of the beet slaw

You could cook the beets if you prefer, but the salad will be sweeter if you do and will lose some of its vital crunch.

Warm steamed cabbage, cream, and mustard. Crisp bacon

Broil bacon till crisp. Lightly steam some coarsely chopped white cabbage leaves and their thick stems. Make a dressing by mixing white wine vinegar, smooth Dijon mustard, olive oil, and a little heavy cream, to taste. Mix the warm drained cabbage with a generous amount of chopped parsley, then toss in the dressing and crumble the crisp bacon on top.

Kohlrabi, blood orange, and coppa

Cut a couple of raw kohlrabi into almost paper-thin slices, then leave to marinate in equal amounts of blood orange juice and white wine vinegar for about an hour. Arrange on a serving plate with thin slices of fat-marbled coppa, black olives, and a little frisée lettuce, crisped in ice-cold water. Finish with finely grated orange zest.

Raw cabbage, blue cheese, cold roast pork

Finely shred equal quantities of raw white and red cabbage and leave to tighten in iced water for 20 minutes. Make a dressing with peanut or canola oil, red wine vinegar, and crumbled blue cheese—I used one part vinegar to two parts oil. Drain the cabbage, then toss with the blue cheese dressing and thin slices of cold roast pork.

Beet and Fennel Slaw with Speck

beet, fennel, speck, sour cream, onion, red wine vinegar

Peel **a large onion**, slice thinly into rings, then put it in a small bowl with **3 tablespoons of red wine vinegar** and set aside for 20 minutes. This will remove the harshness from the raw onion.

Peel **10 ounces (300g) raw beets**—you'll get pink fingers—then slice into the thinnest possible rounds and place in a mixing bowl. Remove the fronds from **2 small fennel bulbs** and set aside, then slice the fennel very finely and add to the beets, but do not mix yet.

Put ⅔ **cup (150ml) sour cream** in a small bowl and beat in **4 tablespoons of olive oil**. Season with salt and black pepper. Drain the onion, discarding the vinegar, and add it to the beets and fennel. Introduce the dressing, slowly and lightly mixing it into the vegetables (overmixing will result in a pink salad).

Pile onto a serving dish, add **6 slices of speck**, and then the reserved fennel fronds.

For 2 to 4. A sweet crunch. The taste of winter.

Crab, Melon, and Basil Salad

crabmeat, melon, red chile, lime, basil

Slice **a lusciously ripe 3-pound (1.5kg) melon** in half and scrape out and discard the seeds. Cut the melon into manageable sections, then remove the flesh from the thick outer skin in short, thick slices. The shape is up to you, but I tend to go for short, finger-thick pieces. Put the melon into a bowl, then seed and very finely shred **a red chile** and place in a small mixing bowl. Pour in **2 tablespoons of olive oil** and **the juice of a ripe lime** and then shred or tear about **12 basil leaves** and mix them in with a little salt and black pepper. Put the melon pieces into the chile and basil dressing and mix together gently, trying not to break the fruit.

Check **8 ounces (250g) lump crabmeat** carefully for any fragments of shell. Place the melon on a serving dish and scatter the crabmeat over the top.

For 2. Shellfish as salty, fresh, and bracing as a wave. Sweet, juicy melon.

Cucumber, Fennel, and Ricotta Salad

cucumber, fennel, ricotta, avocado, lemon, balsamic vinegar, dill, sprouts

Make the dressing: Put **2 tablespoons of lemon juice** in a bowl, stir in a little salt and black pepper, then whisk in **2 tablespoons of olive oil** and **2 tablespoons of sunflower oil**. Add **a few drops of balsamic vinegar**. Finely chop **3 or 4 sprigs of dill** and add to the dressing, then taste and check the balance. It should be fresh but not sharp. Add more balsamic vinegar as necessary.

Peel **half a cucumber**, remove the seeds with a teaspoon, then cut it into thick slices. Halve and finely slice **a small bulb of fennel**. Peel and thickly slice **an avocado** and fold all gently into the dressing, then let everything sit in a cool place for about half an hour (not much longer though). Add **several tufts of sprouts**, such as radish or mung bean.

Transfer to a serving dish, place **a large spoonful of ricotta** per person on top, and serve.

For 2. Light, bright, refreshing. A mild, gentle salad.

Some ideas for mozzarella

The classic

There are few salads as sublime as mozzarella, basil, and tomato, but I like mine dressed with olive oil that you have blitzed to a thin puree with basil leaves and a dash of red wine vinegar.

With roast tomatoes and thyme

Halve small, ripe tomatoes, drizzle with olive oil, then season with thyme, rosemary, salt, and pepper and cook under a broiler. Tuck torn pieces of mozzarella among them.

Crumbed and fried

Slice the mozzarella thickly. Dip in seasoned, beaten egg and bread crumbs, then fry in olive oil till crisp. Lemon wedges. Maybe some thick slices of ripe tomato.

Pancetta-Crumbed
Mozzarella Salad

smoked pancetta, mozzarella, tomatoes,
lettuce, basil

Broil or fry **12 thin slices of smoked pancetta** till very crisp, drain
briefly on paper towels, then puree to coarse crumbs in a food
processor. Break **a large ball of buffalo mozzarella** into 4 pieces,
then roll in the pancetta crumbs.

Slice and lightly salt **2 large tomatoes** and place on a plate with
4 small leaves of butterhead lettuce. Puree ½ **cup (10g) basil** with
5 tablespoons of olive oil and a little salt and pepper. Place the
crumbed mozzarella on the tomatoes and lettuce, then spoon over
the basil dressing.

For 2 as a light lunch. Crisp pancetta, soft mozzarella.

A few options for peas and cheese

Peas and cheese 1

Add raw fresh peas to a salad of watercress and sliced oranges. Crumble feta cheese on top and add some fruity olive oil.

Peas and cheese 2

Grate Parmesan cheese into some freshly cooked warm peas and toss with melted butter or olive oil. The cheese will melt very slightly. Great with lamb chops.

Peas and cheese 3

Toss freshly cooked hot peas and skinned fava beans with a firm white cheese such as Ticklemore or Ryefield goat. Throw in some sliced radishes and add an olive oily–lemony dressing.

Peas and Ham

peas, ham, pine nuts, red pepper
flakes, pea shoots

Pod **7 ounces (200g) fresh peas**; if you have bought them already
podded, you will need ⅔ cup (100g). Put them in a large bowl.
Coarsely chop **3 tablespoons of pine nuts** and put them in a shallow
pan with **a teaspoon of red pepper flakes** and **3½ tablespoons (50g)
butter**. Let the pine nuts color a little.

Tear **5 ounces (150g) thick-sliced cooked ham** into rough, jagged
pieces, add them to the raw peas, and dress with the hot pine nut
butter. Top with **a large handful of pea shoots**, if you have them.

For 2. Humble, sweet. A fresh hit of green peas.

A couple of thoughts on the corn salad

- Raw corn, which I have used here, is less sugary than cooked and has a more satisfying crunch.
- Whole heads of corn can be peeled, basted with maple syrup and butter, and roasted. Turn them from time to time as they cook, then serve with an endive and toasted pecan salad.

Corn, Bacon, and Parsley Salad

corn on the cob, bacon, parsley,
roasted salted almonds

Heat **3 tablespoons of olive oil** in a shallow pan. Slice **4 slices bacon** into long, thin strips and fry in the oil till almost crisp. Add **⅓ cup (50g) roasted, salted almonds** and continue cooking for a minute or two. Slice the kernels off **a corn cob** and stir them into the bacon. Mix briefly, so the raw corn is coated with the bacon fat, then toss with **a handful of torn parsley leaves** and serve immediately.

For 2. Sweet, salty, and crunchy.

A few thoughts on the couscous

- A frugal way to use up the spare meat from the Sunday roast, this is also a clever way to celebrate the remains of the Christmas turkey or goose. I pull the poultry meat from its bones in large, bite-size pieces and only at the last minute to keep it moist and juicy.
- Instant couscous doesn't need cooking. Pour an equal volume of boiling water over the grains and leave for 10 minutes, until the water has been absorbed, then fluff it up with a fork.
- Pomegranate molasses, with its sweet-sour, caramel citrus tang, is available from Middle Eastern grocers and major supermarkets.

Other ideas for couscous

Torn ham, parsley, green lentils, the rough crunch of russet apples

Tear rough, bite-size pieces of ham into the prepared couscous. Stir through golden raisins, chopped parsley, cooked and drained Puy lentils, and slices of crisp, cold, slightly tart apple.

Roast pork, chilled tangerines, cool mint

Tear pieces of cold roast pork left from the Sunday roast into chunky pieces. Stir them through the soaked and fluffed couscous. Add peeled and sliced tangerines, parsley, and shredded mint leaves; no dried fruits but perhaps some of the pomegranate seeds and pistachios.

Turkey or Chicken Couscous

leftover cooked turkey or chicken or goose, couscous, pumpkin seeds, dried cranberries, golden raisins, pistachios, mint, pomegranate, yogurt, pomegranate molasses

Pour **2 cups (480ml) of boiling water** over **a cup (200g) of couscous**, cover with a lid, then leave to plump up until the water has been fully absorbed. Shred **1¼ pounds (600g) cooked turkey, chicken**, or **goose** into large, juicy pieces and put it into a mixing bowl with **2 tablespoons of pumpkin seeds, 2 tablespoons of dried cranberries or cherries, 2 tablespoons of golden raisins**, and **2 tablespoons of shelled pistachios**. Season generously with salt, pepper, and **chopped mint leaves**, then add **the seeds of a whole pomegranate**.

Fluff up the couscous with a fork, then fold in the dry ingredients. Top with **4 heaping tablespoons of yogurt, a trickle of pomegranate molasses**, more **mint leaves**, and **a few more pomegranate seeds**.

For 2 to 3. Bejeweled leftovers.

A few thoughts on the vegetables with couscous

- Use instant couscous. If you have the traditional variety, steam it till tender.
- You can grill the vegetables, if you prefer, or cook them in a shallow pan on the stove. Make sure the vegetables are still warm when you dress them. The vegetables could include zucchini and marinated eggplant (olive oil, garlic). You could also put the cooked vegetables on bruschetta. It would be more of a snack, but still worth a go.
- Swap the couscous for cracked wheat or rice if you prefer.

For a change

A cheese and apple couscous

Swell the couscous in hot apple juice. Toss with toasted walnuts, shredded fennel, Cheshire cheese, cubed apples, and lots of freshly chopped parsley. A little black pepper, a pinch (no more) of ground cinnamon, and a squeeze of lemon to finish.

Ham and fava beans, mild flavors for a summer's day

Boil a small (1-pound / 500g) ham hock in water for about 40 minutes, till tender. Remove from the cooking liquid and set aside. Pour the liquid into a bowl, add the couscous, cover, and let it swell. Remove the ham from the bone and toss with young fava beans, sliced fennel, and chopped parsley. A little olive oil will moisten it nicely.

An herb and arugula couscous

Pour the couscous into a heatproof bowl and add a tablespoon of olive oil. Add boiling water or stock, cover, and leave to swell. Toss together a mixture of toasted pine nuts, fried finely sliced onions, and an abundance of chopped dill, parsley, and mint. The quantity of herbs to couscous should be about equal. Fold the mixture together with handfuls of arugula leaves.

Summer Vegetables with Harissa and Couscous

couscous, cherry tomatoes, red onion,
harissa paste, vegetable stock

Halve **7 ounces (200g) mixed cherry tomatoes** and put into a
roasting pan. Peel and slice **a red onion** and add to the tomatoes.
Toss the vegetables gently in **olive oil** to coat evenly, then bake at
400°F (200°C) for approximately 20 minutes, till the tomatoes have
started to burst and the onions are soft enough to crush between
your fingers. Pour ½ **cup (100g) couscous** into the roasting pan.

Bring 1⅔ **cups (400ml) vegetable stock** to a boil, pour over the
couscous, cover tightly with foil, then leave for 15 minutes. Season
the couscous with black pepper, then stir in **a tablespoon of harissa
paste**. Serve the couscous with the roast vegetables.

For 2. Grains to nourish and enliven.

Figs, Bulgur, and Blackberries

figs, bulgur wheat, blackberries, walnut oil,
red wine vinegar

Bring **1 cup (150g) bulgur wheat** to a boil in a large pot of lightly
salted water, then cover the pan, turn off the heat, and leave for about
20 minutes, till tender.

Take **5 ounces (150g) blackberries** and crush 4 of them in a
bowl with a fork. Stir in **a tablespoon of walnut (or olive) oil** and
2 tablespoons of red wine vinegar. Wipe **3 ripe figs**, cut off the
stalks, then slice down from tip to base a few times, not quite cutting
through to the bottom. Press the sides gently to open each fig out
like a flower.

Drain any water from the bulgur, then toss the wheat with the
remaining blackberries, the blackberry dressing, and the figs.

For 3. Calm grain, bright, fruity dressing. A side dish for ham or
beef, or a light lunch.

A few ideas for beef dripping

With rosemary, on toast

Very hot, crisp sourdough toast, spread generously but not gluttonously with beef dripping, a pinch of very finely chopped rosemary, and, should you have some, a smear of roasted garlic.

Slow-baked peppers

Melt beef dripping in a roasting pan, add a few Italian sweet peppers, halved lengthwise, and slow roast till they are soft as silk. Pile onto toasted sourdough bread with a handful of arugula.

Onion confit in beef dripping with melted cheese

Warm some dripping in a shallow pan, then add sliced onions and cook over moderate heat till they are soft, golden, and sticky. Stir in some of the dark jelly that lies under the fat, then, as it starts to bubble, add chunks of fontina cheese and let them melt into golden pools. Don't stir, but spoon the strings of soft onions, molten cheese, and beef juices onto rough, artisan-type toast.

Beef Dripping Potato Salad

beef dripping, new potatoes, egg yolks, arugula or watercress, leftover Sunday roast beef

Halve, but don't peel, **12 ounces (350g) new potatoes** and boil until tender. Drain and leave to cool. Warm **5 ounces (150g) beef dripping** in a small pan to melt it. Put **2 egg yolks** in a mixing bowl, then beat in the warm beef fat a little at a time, as if you were making mayonnaise. You will need to do this with a handheld electric mixer on high speed. It simply won't work otherwise. When the mayonnaise is thick, add the cooled potatoes and a little salt.

Serve on a bed of **arugula or watercress**, then top with the crisp end of the Sunday roast, **a few slices of rare leftover beef**, and the brown residue and sediment, warmed a little, from the roasting pan.

For 2. Deeply savory, salty, almost smoky. A sensational end for the roast.

Other accompaniments to crispbreads

Feta and cucumber

Grated cucumber, black pepper, chopped mint, a few capers, and some roughly crumbled feta cheese. Fold gently through thick sheep's or goat's milk yogurt and pile onto crispbreads. Clean, piquant, bright.

Pork pâté and apricots

A rough mound of coarse pork or goose rillettes, a few salted capers, and slices of ripe, fresh, but still slightly sharp apricot.

Chickpea and anchovies

Add a drained 14-ounce (400g) can of chickpeas to a food processor and add 8 anchovy fillets, a good squeeze or two of lemon juice, and a handful of flat-leaf parsley. Puree, introducing a few tablespoons of olive oil as you go, till you have a coarse, soft paste. Pile onto crispbreads.

Salmon with Roast Garlic and Cream

smoked salmon, garlic, cream, dill, crispbreads

Preheat the oven to 400°F (200°C). Bake **a head of garlic** for 30 to 40 minutes, until soft. Squeeze the soft cloves out of their skins into a bowl with your finger and thumb. Gently whisk in ⅔ **cup (150ml) heavy cream**. Chop **4 ounces (110g) dill** (you can do this in a food processor, but give only 3 very short bursts on the pulse button). Stir the dill into the garlic cream. Get **10 ounces (300g) smoked salmon** near. Top **crispbreads** with pieces of salmon and dollops of dressing.

For 2 to 4. Silky salmon. Crisp bread.

Some thoughts on the tomatoes with anchovy

- Ripe, sweet tomatoes are best for this, to balance the salty qualities of the anchovies.
- You don't need to put salt on the tomatoes; the anchovies are salt enough.
- Use chervil in place of the basil.
- Serve the whole lot as a filling for warm pita, scooping the cooked tomatoes and crunchy cucumber into toasted pita pockets.
- Add a crumbling of feta cheese and a few torn basil leaves.

Tomatoes, Cucumber, and Anchovy

tomatoes, cucumber, anchovy fillets, tarragon, basil, parsley

Slice **4 large tomatoes** in half and put them on a baking sheet. Drizzle with **a little olive oil** and season with black pepper. Take **8 anchovy fillets** and add one to each tomato half. Cook under a broiler till hot and lightly toasted.

Peel **a cucumber**, slice down its length, then scrape out the seeds with a teaspoon and discard. Chop the cucumber into thick chunks. Make a dressing for the cucumber by pouring **5 tablespoons of olive oil** into a blender or food processor, adding the leaves from **3 or 4 large sprigs of tarragon, 5 large basil leaves**, and **a few parsley leaves** and pureeing till you have a bright green dressing. Season with salt and pepper and toss with the cucumber.

For 2. Vibrant, refreshing.

A few thoughts on the cherries and salami

- Sweet-sharp fruits and soft, flat speckled salami make a fine addition to a summer lunch.
- The salad will be at its best if the cherries are cold from the fridge and the tomatoes are not overripe, maybe even slightly sharp. It can also be served as a starter.
- Mozzarella would work well in this salad too.

Cherries, Tomatoes, and Salami

cherries, cherry tomatoes,
salami, tarragon vinegar

Halve and pit **5 ounces (150g) ripe cherries**. Cut **5 ounces (150g) cherry tomatoes** in half, then toss them with the cherries. Sprinkle **a little tarragon vinegar** on top and set aside for no longer than half an hour. The fruits don't need to be seasoned.

Slice **3½ ounces (100g) good, peppery salami** very thinly and remove the casing, then tuck among the cherries and tomatoes.

For 2. Light, bright, the taste of summer.

A few thoughts on the potatoes and speck

- I use speck for the salad opposite because its flavor holds up well against the broccoli, but you could use any air-dried meat.
- This is also a good way of using up the Sunday roast. Cut the slices as thinly as possible.
- For a less rich version, make a dressing with olive oil, lemon juice, and dill instead of the crème fraîche.
- After slicing the potatoes in half, I sometimes toss them in a little sizzling oil or butter to crisp them.

For when asparagus are available

An asparagus and ham salad

Boil or steam asparagus spears, drain them, then add them to the salad opposite instead of the broccoli. I prefer to use chervil or tarragon for this, though dill, basil, or fennel fronds will also work.

Potatoes, Speck, and Broccoli Rabe

new potatoes, speck, broccoli rabe, dill,
crème fraîche

Scrub **12 ounces (350g) new potatoes**. Bring a large pot of water to a boil, salt it, then add the potatoes and cook for 20 minutes or so, till tender. Drain the potatoes and cut them in half. Finely chop **a few fronds of dill** and stir into ⅔ **cup (150ml) crème fraîche** together with a little salt and pepper. Gently toss the hot potatoes in this dressing.

Trim **3½ ounces (100g) broccoli rabe**, keeping the most tender leaves attached, then steam or cook in lightly salted boiling water for a few minutes, till done to your liking. Drain and toss carefully with the potatoes, trying not to break the spears up. Serve on plates or in shallow bowls, tucking **3½ ounces (100g) thinly cut speck** in among the potatoes and broccoli.

For 2. Broccoli, smoked ham, dill potatoes. Substantial.

Desserts

Most weekday meals, at least in our house, end with a piece of fruit or a slice of cake. It may be a ripe white peach or a bowl of raspberries. It could be a bulging fig, a pear, and a piece of Parmesan, or a plate of cherries with a slice of goat cheese. Many is the time I have closed a meal with some fine chocolate or some store-bought ice cream. There might be Turkish delight or possibly a handful or two of almonds I have tossed in sugar and left to caramelize in a shallow pan.

But sometimes there has to be a proper dessert. A cheesecake, a trifle, a crumble, or a meringue. Indulgent, wholly unnecessary food of a sweet and sugary kind. That ripe peach could be sliced and dropped into a glass of muscat; the raspberries could be pureed and used as a sauce for ice cream or strawberries. The figs could be baked with a glass of Marsala and some brown sugar. But sometimes, there just has to be dessert.

I like the idea of baking a banana in its skin till it blackens, splitting it open, and squeezing a ripe passion fruit inside, just as I am all for a baked apple if the oven is on anyway. But there are other shortcuts too:

Blackberries, red wine

Bring a few glasses of red wine to a boil, add a tablespoon of sugar for each one, and drop in about 14 ounces (400g) blackberries. Cook for a few minutes, till the fruit starts to soften, then eat warm.

Baked apples, passion fruit

Score some small apples around their middles and bake at 400°F (200°C) for 25 minutes, until they are soft. As they come from the oven, squeeze passion fruit juice and seeds over them. Serve with cream.

Bananas, yogurt, cream

Peel 4 very ripe, soft bananas and puree them in a food processor. Scrape into a bowl, then fold in ⅔ cup (150ml) thick, sharp yogurt and an equal amount of very softly whipped heavy cream. Spoon into glasses and chill.

Raspberries and cream

Make a chilled raspberry fool by putting 10 ounces (300g) frozen raspberries into a food processor with 1 cup (250ml) heavy cream. Puree briefly. You will have something between fool and ice cream.

Blackberry panettone

Toast slices of panettone till golden. Spread generously with a mixture of mascarpone and softly whipped cream. Pile with blackberries, then dust with confectioners' sugar.

A chocolate sandwich

Grate chocolate generously onto slices of brioche, then sandwich together. Toast on both sides in a shallow pan till the chocolate melts. Dust with confectioners' sugar and eat. (Nutella works too, if you have no chocolate.)

Raspberry ripple sandwich
Crush a mixture of raspberries and blackberries with a fork. Sweeten some softly whipped cream with a little confectioners' sugar and vanilla extract. Toast some brioche or plain white bread till pale gold. Fold the crushed berries lightly through the cream in dark red streaks. Pile onto the crisp, warm toast.

An ice cream sandwich
Take 2 thin, crumbly oatmeal or shortbread cookies. Pile with vanilla ice cream, then add a scattering of dark chocolate smashed into thin shards. Put another cookie on top of each and press together lightly. Return briefly to the freezer before eating.

Banana Cheesecake

bananas, gingersnaps, butter, heavy cream,
white chocolate, cream cheese, vanilla, lemon

To make the crumb crust, melt **4 tablespoons (60g) butter** in a small
saucepan and add **3 tablespoons of heavy cream**. Crush **10 ounces
(275g) gingersnaps** in a food processor, then stir into the melted butter
mixture. When all the crumbs are moist, set about 3 tablespoons of
them aside, then transfer the rest to an 8-inch (20cm) springform cake
pan and smooth them gently, but avoid compacting them. You want a
loose, crumbly crust.

To make the filling, place a heatproof bowl over a saucepan of
simmering water, making sure the water doesn't touch the bottom of
the bowl. Break **7 ounces (200g) white chocolate** into small pieces and
drop them into the bowl, leaving them, unstirred, to melt. As soon as
the chocolate has melted, turn off the heat, pour in ¾ **cup (200ml)
heavy cream** and add **a couple of drops of vanilla extract**. Slowly stir
the cream and chocolate together.

Tip 1¼ **pounds (600g) cream cheese** into a bowl and fold the white
chocolate and cream mixture into it. Scoop the filling on top of the
crumb crust, smooth the surface level, then cover with plastic wrap
and refrigerate for at least 3 hours.

continued

Banana Cheesecake, *continued*

To finish, peel and slice **3 bananas**, toss them in **the juice of a lemon**, then pile them on top of the chilled cheesecake. Scatter over the reserved crumbs (if they have set, simply break them up first).

For 8. Creamy, vanilla scent, ginger crumbs.

A few thoughts on the strawberry salad

I know the salad opposite sounds unusual, but it is the crispest, most refreshing fruit salad imaginable. The strawberries and cucumber work beautifully with the syrup. This is summer in a bowl.

More unusual salads

- Peeled lychees tossed with raspberries.
- Blackberries, raspberries, and ripe black currants.
- Watermelon, loganberries, and a syrup made from sugar, water, and mint.
- Peaches, raspberries, the faintest breath of rose water.
- Mango and passion fruit, perfect partners.

Strawberry and Cucumber Salad

strawberries, cucumbers, honey, mint, elderflower syrup

Put **3 tablespoons of honey, 10 mint leaves**, and **5 tablespoons of elderflower syrup** into a blender and puree to a thick, fragrant syrup. (If you don't have a blender, chop the mint very, very finely, mix it with the honey and syrup, then leave it for an hour. Strain through a fine-mesh sieve or cheesecloth to remove the mint.)

Peel **2 medium cucumbers**, slice them in half lengthwise, then scrape the seeds out with a teaspoon. Dice the flesh finely and put it in a large bowl. Remove the leaves from **1 pound (450g) strawberries**, then slice the fruit in half and toss gently with the cucumber.

Pour the mint and elderflower syrup onto the fruit, stir very gently, then cover and leave in the fridge for about 30 minutes before serving.

For 4 to 6. The essence of summer, like Pimm's on perfectly mown grass.

Chocolate Oat Crumble

dark chocolate, rolled oats, maple syrup,
apricots, raspberries, elderflower syrup

Preheat the oven to 350°F (180°C). Chop **1½ ounces (40g) dark chocolate** and mix it with **½ cup (50g) rolled oats** and **5 tablespoons of maple syrup**.

Halve and pit **6 apricots** and place them in a shallow ovenproof pan. Drizzle with **4 tablespoons of elderflower syrup**. Let the liquid bubble over moderate heat for 3 or 4 minutes, then add **5 ounces (150g) raspberries**.

Scatter the oat mixture over the fruit and bake for 20 minutes, till the fruit is soft and fragrant and the oats crisp.

For 3. Heady, crisp, luscious.

Irish Coffee Trifle

ladyfingers, Baileys Irish Cream, espresso,
hazelnuts, heavy cream, mascarpone, vanilla,
dark chocolate

Put **3½ ounces (100g) ladyfingers** into a serving bowl and pour over
⅔ cup (150ml) Baileys Irish Cream and **⅔ cup (150ml) strong espresso
coffee**. Leave to soak. Toast **¾ cup (100g) skinned hazelnuts** and chop
them in half. Whip **¾ cup (200ml) heavy cream** to soft folds, then fold
in **¾ cup (200g) mascarpone cheese** and most of the chopped hazelnuts.
Spread the hazelnut mixture over the ladyfingers and refrigerate.

Softly whip another **¾ cup (200ml) heavy cream**, flavor it with
a little vanilla extract or a knifepoint of vanilla seeds, then spread it
over the hazelnut and mascarpone cream. Leave, covered, in the
fridge for about an hour (20 minutes will do in a trifle emergency).

Scatter the remaining hazelnuts over the cream. Melt **1¼ ounces
(35g) dark chocolate** in a small bowl set over a pan of simmering
water, then drizzle and splatter the chocolate over the surface of the
cream. Refrigerate for a few minutes, till the chocolate turns crisp,
then bring to the table.

For 6. Deep layers of bliss.

A few thoughts on the oat cookies

- If you eat these cookies within an hour of filling, they will remain crisp. But I prefer them the next day, when they become soft and chewy.
- Rather than filling the cookies with the lemon cream, melt 3½ ounces (100g) dark chocolate, dip each cookie halfway into the chocolate, then leave on waxed paper in a cool place to set. Alternatively, drizzle melted chocolate randomly over the cookies (in which case you will need a little less chocolate).
- Crumble the cooled cookies over vanilla ice cream.
- Sandwich the cookies together with vanilla ice cream instead of lemon curd and mascarpone, returning them briefly to the freezer to set.

Oat and Lemon Cookies

oats, butter, muscovado sugar, egg yolk, flour,
baking powder, mascarpone, lemon curd

Preheat the oven to 350°F (180°C). Dice ½ **cup (120g) softened butter**
and, using an electric mixer, beat with ½ **cup (120g) packed muscovado
sugar** till light and creamy. Beat in **an egg yolk**. Mix in together **1⅓ cups
(120g) old-fashioned rolled oats, ¾ cup (90g) all-purpose flour, half a
teaspoon of baking powder**, and a generous pinch of sea salt.

Divide the mixture into 8 to 12 pieces, depending on how large you
would like your cookies to be. Roll into balls, then flatten each one out
into a disk about 2½ inches (6cm) in diameter and place them on a
baking sheet lined with parchment paper. They should be quite thick,
so they remain a little chewy after baking.

Bake the cookies for 12 to 15 minutes, till they are lightly colored but
not yet crisp. Remove the baking sheet from the oven, leave to cool
for a minute or two, then transfer the cookies to a wire cooling rack.
As they cool, they will crisp up.

To make the filling, put **scant ½ cup (100g) mascarpone cheese** in a
mixing bowl and stir in ½ **cup (100g) lemon curd**. Use to sandwich the
cookies together.

Makes 4 to 6.

Strawberry Mascarpone Brioche Toasts

strawberries, mascarpone, brioche, hazelnuts,
sugar, vanilla extract, heavy cream

Lightly oil a nonstick baking sheet, using a mild or flavorless oil. Put
⅓ cup (40g) skinned hazelnuts and ⅓ cup (80g) superfine sugar in a
nonstick frying pan with a couple of tablespoons of water and bring to
a boil. Let the mixture bubble until the nuts are pale gold. Do not stir
more than once or twice. Watch them carefully as the color darkens
a little, then spread them on the prepared baking sheet. Leave for
10 minutes to cool and crisp.

Slice 20 strawberries in half. You can remove the leaves if you wish.
Lightly whip ¾ cup (200ml) heavy cream till thick, then gently fold in
¾ cup (200g) mascarpone cheese and a little vanilla extract. Coarsely
chop the sugared hazelnuts and fold half of them into the cream and
mascarpone.

Toast 4 slices of brioche and spread some of the mascarpone
cream on each slice. Pile the strawberries on top and scatter with the
reserved chopped sugared nuts.

For 4. Soft, sweet toast, berries, cream. Summer.

Mango and Passion Fruit Mess

mangoes, passion fruits, heavy cream, meringue

Whip **1¼ cups (300ml) heavy cream** till it stands in soft folds. Crumble **6 ounces (180g) store-bought or homemade meringues** into it, roughly, so you get both large and small pieces, but do not stir.

Peel **2 small, very ripe honey mangoes**, slice the flesh from the pits, and chop it into small pieces. Add to the cream and meringues. Halve **6 ripe passion fruits**, then squeeze out the juice through a small sieve into a bowl. Gently, very gently, fold the juice, mango, and meringues into the whipped cream. It will need only 2 or 3 stirs at most. You can chill for an hour or so, if you wish.

For 4. Heavenly assembly.

Fig and Ricotta Toasts

figs, ricotta, raisin bread, heavy cream,
walnuts, honey, rosemary

Put **4 tablespoons of shelled walnuts** into a shallow pan and add
2 tablespoons of honey and **a bushy sprig of rosemary**, crushing it
in your hand a little as you do. Let the honey bubble for a minute or
two till it starts to darken slightly, then remove from the heat and
set aside for 10 minutes.

Slice **2 perfectly ripe figs** in half. Stir **4 tablespoons of heavy cream**
into **4 tablespoons of ricotta**. Lightly toast **2 slices of raisin bread**.

Place the toast on 2 plates, divide the ricotta cream between them,
place figs on each, then spoon the warm walnuts and honey on top.

For 2. Figs, ricotta, honey, and rosemary. Ancient flavors.
Contemporary twist.

Index

A

almonds

anchovies

apples

apricots

artichokes, globe

artichokes, Jerusalem

arugula

asparagus

avocados

B

K

L

N

naan

Cannellini mash, butter and spices, warm naan 175

Spiced mushrooms on naan 221

noodles

Chicken, asparagus, and noodle broth 59

The deep savor of beef and noodle broth 45

Greens and bean sprouts. The warmth of coconut and noodles 54

The otherworldliness of squid, the homeliness of udon noodles 344

Pork belly with lime and Sichuan peppercorns 351

Pure, clear chicken noodle soup 344

Roast chicken pho 65

Shrimp, noodles, and spring carrots 345

Soba noodles, salmon, and shrimp 353

Summer herb rolls 15

O

oats

Chocolate oat crumble 403

Oat and lemon cookies 407

olives

Anchovies, olives, and basil croutons, a salad for high summer 228

Basil, pine nuts, garlic, mozzarella, and lemon-scented olives with couscous 358

Lamb with black garlic and olives 157

Lamb with za'atar and olives 157

Tuna and cucumber salad 361

onions

Black bean and onion stew 247

Caramelized onions, Parmesan, capers 288

Cheese and onion mash 198

Chicken wing onion broth 58

Chicken wings with onion umeboshi chutney 163

Classic sausage, cloud-like mash, sweet onion gravy 90

Classic sausage and mash 290

Grilled duck and red onions 114

A hash-brown crust 322

Lamb's liver, onions, and pecorino 107

Lentils and golden onions, smoked bacon, crème fraîche 182

Onion confit in beef dripping with melted cheese on toast 384

Onion and mushroom toad in the hole 307

Onion, quince paste, and blue cheese sandwich 24

Poor man's potatoes 113

Roasted vegetable rice 227

Root vegetable tangle 311

Rumbledethumps 198

Sweet onions and sausage sandwich 28

Tomatoes, charred onions, and steak 141

oranges

Chicken with orange and sherry vinegar 278

Kohlrabi, blood orange, and coppa 366

Pork with blood orange 305

Squash with chile and orange 248

P

pancetta

Asparagus, bacon, Parmesan 296

Black bean and onion stew 247

Chicken breast with pancetta and mustard 272

Chicken breast with smoked cheese and pancetta 273

Monkfish with pancetta and clams 105

Pancetta, salmon, crisp baguette 180

Pancetta-crumbed mozzarella salad 373

paneer cheese

Eggplant paneer 109

panettone

Blackberry panettone 396

A note on the type

Typeset in Nexus Mix, a slab serif created by Dutch type designer Martin Majoor in 2004. Nexus is a highly legible, humanistic typeface which takes its name from the Latin word for connection.